SCOTTISH HIGHLANDERS ON THE EVE
OF THE
GREAT MIGRATION
1725 - 1775

THE PEOPLE OF THE GRAMPIAN HIGHLANDS

Volume II

Balmoral Castle from the river

SCOTTISH HIGHLANDERS ON THE EVE OF THE GREAT MIGRATION 1725 - 1775

THE PEOPLE OF THE GRAMPIAN HIGHLANDS

Volume II

Copyright © 2019
by David Dobson
All Rights Reserved

Printed for Clearfield Company by
Genealogical Publishing Company
Baltimore, Maryland
2019

ISBN 9780806358888

INTRODUCTION

Emigration from Scotland to colonial America, which had been small scale during the seventeenth century, became significant during the eighteenth century. Much of this exodus originated in the Highlands of Scotland where the traditional social and economic structures were beginning to break down under pressure from the Commercial and the Industrial Revolutions transpiring in both England and Lowland Scotland. Profits were to be made by supplying raw materials and foodstuffs to the growing factory towns. Clan chiefs increasingly abandoned their patriarchal role in favour of becoming capitalist landlords, and the traditional social fabric of the Highlands was soon in tatters. This social breakdown was intensified through the failure of the Jacobite cause in 1746, followed by the military occupation and repression that occurred in the Highlands in the aftermath of their defeat at Culloden. The great Highland landowners and clan chiefs, now absorbed into the British elite, increased farm rents in order to maintain their new lifestyles.

Voluntary emigration by Gaelic-speaking Highlanders began in the 1730s when some groups left Argyll bound for North Carolina and New York, and others vacated Inverness bound for Georgia. In 1746 the British Government despatched about one thousand Jacobite prisoners of war, in chains, as indentured servants bound for the colonies. During the Seven Years War, 1756 to 1763, Highland Regiments were raised for the first time. In North America, accordingly, this military struggle between Britain and France (known as the French and Indian War) saw regiments such as Fraser's Highlanders and Montgomery's Highlanders play a significant role. Many of these veterans chose to settle in the former French Canada and in America rather than return to Scotland. These military settlers, and their families and friends who followed, formed a substantial portion of the Highlanders who settled in the years before the outbreak of the American Revolution in 1776. The 1760s and early 1770s were the peak periods for Highland emigration in the eighteenth century. After 1783 the emphasis of Highland settlement was in Canada although emigration to America continued to a lesser degree. Yet another cause of Highland emigration was the pressure that a significant population increase placed on the region's limited resources.

What resources are available to those wishing to trace their immigrant ancestors of the eighteenth century from the Highlands of Scotland? The most important genealogical sources are the Old Parish Registers of the Church of Scotland, which provide data on baptisms and marriages. While this is generally successful for eighteenth-century research covering Lowland Scotland, there are severe limitations on their use for Highland research. The registers for members of the Church of Scotland, in and of themselves, are incomplete for the Highlands. A number of Highlanders, moreover, were Roman Catholic or Episcopalian. Prior to 1788, these individuals were subject to Penal Law restrictions, because of their links with Jacobitism, and consequently have only partial records. In the absence of church records, family historians have to turn to a miscellany of other records, such as court records, estate papers, sasines, gravestone inscriptions, burgess rolls, port books, services of heirs, wills and testaments, and particularly rent rolls. The latter source establishes which family was settled on which farm at a specific period in time and provides a site for genealogists to link to.

This volume is the second in this series to deal with the Grampian Highlands, an area which stretches from the Braes of Angus north-westwards towards Strathspey but does not include the fertile coastal plain nor Strathmore. Since the north-east of Scotland tended to be a stronghold of Jacobitism, many of its supporters from the Grampian Highlands were transported in chains, banished to America and the West Indies. By the late eighteenth century the rise of the transatlantic timber trade enabled many from the region voluntarily to emigrate, notably via Aberdeen to the Canadian Maritimes.

David Dobso

Dundee, Scotland, 2019

SCOTTISH HIGHLANDERS, 1725-1775; GRAMPIAN HIGHLANDS, II

REFERENCES

ACA = Aberdeen City Archives

CAT = Chronicles of Atholl and Tullibardine

DPD = Diocese and Presbytery of Dunkeld

DUAS = Dundee University Archival Service

EMA = Emigrant Ministers to America

F = Fasti Ecclesiae Scoticanae

FPA = Fulham Papers, American

HM = History of Maryland

LPR = List of Persons in the Rebellion

NRS = National Records of Scotland

OR = Muster Roll of Lord Ogilvy's Regiment

SHS = Scottish History Society

SPC = State Papers, Colonial

SRS = Scottish Records Society

SSPCK = Scottish Society Promation of Christian Knowledge

SAUL = St Andrews University Library

TNA = The National Archives, Kew

Bridge over Sluggan Water, near Braemar.

Dr. Guthrie's house, Loch Lee.

ABERCROMBY, GEORGE, was granted the lands of Banchory, Aberdeenshire, in 1733. [NRS.SIG1.4.71]

ABERCROMBY, RALPH, was granted the lands of Banchory, Aberdeenshire, in 1758. [NRS.SIG1.5.64]

ABERNETHY, ALEXANDER, born 1777, farmer at Nether Tillylair, died 6 October 1826. [Strachan gravestone]

ADAM, JAMES, minister at Cortachy, a sasine, 1710. [NRS.RS35.12.238]

ADAM, JOHN, born 1695, farmer at Strichmoir, died 17 February 1760?, husband of Katherine Troup, parents of John born 1747, died April 1767, Ann born 1727, died August 1752, Rachel born 1742, died March 1764, Janet died in infancy. [Strachan, Kincardineshire, gravestone]

ADAM, JOHN, in Milton of Blacklunan, Angus, 1710. [NRS.RS35.12.353]

ADAMSON, JAMES, in Kirkton of Kingoldrum, testament, 1738, Comm. Brechin. [NRS]

ADAMSON, JAMES, a farmer in Kingoldrum, a Jacobite in 1745. [OR.8]

ADAMSON, JOHN, at the Milne of Blacklunans, Angus, husband of Magdalene Farquharson, sasine, 1704. [NRS.RS35.10/532]

ADAMSON, JOHN, a brewer in Kirkton of Airlie, Angus, 1774. [NRS.GD16.Sec.28/374]

ADAMSON, JOHN, in Greenmire, Kinnordy, Angus, 1755. [NRS.GD205.29.239]

AITKEN, JOHN, in Westerton of Strathcathro, Angus, testament, 1738, Comm. Brechin. [NRS]

ALEXANDER, ELIZABETH, daughter of Reverend John Alexander in Kildrummy, Aberdeenshire, and Alexander Adie, son of the deceased John Adie deacon convenor of Dunfermline, an ante nuptial marriage contract, 1719. [NRS.CH12.33.10]

ALEXANDER, JAMES, a ploughman at Gairlaw, Lintrathen, a Jacobite in 1745. [OR.11]

ALEXANDER, JOHN, minister at Kildrummy, Aberdeenshire, a letter, 1712, [NRS.CH12.12.66]; and his spouse Anna Gordon, a deed, 1716. [NRS.CH12.33.7]

ALEXANDER, JOHN, son of Reverend John Alexander minister at Kildrummy, Aberdeenshire, and his relict Anna Gordon, a deed, 1722. [NRS.CH12.23.15]

ALEXANDER, JOHN, in the Old Mill of Fern, Angus, a sasine, 1775. [NRS.RS35.25.467]

ALEXANDER, MARGARET, daughter of Reverend John Alexander in Kildrummy, Aberdeenshire, and Thomas Kirkwood schoolmaster of Cranston, an ante nuptial marriage contract, 1719. [NRS.CH12.33.11]

ALEXANDER, SOPHIA, daughter of Reverend John Alexander in Kildrummy, Aberdeenshire, and John Gordon in Newton of Achindore, an ante nuptial marriage contract, 1719. [NRS.CH12.33.12]

ALLAN, DAVID, in Inch, Cadham, Kinnordy, Angus, 1755. [NRS.GD205.29.239]

ALLAN, JOHN, a workman in Pitmody, Lintrathen, Angus, a Jacobite in 1745. [OR.11]

ANDERSON, ALEXANDER, born 1715, tenant in Cranore, died 19 January 1777, husband of Agnes Jaffrey, born 1713, died 11 January 1775. [Kincardine O'Neil gravestone]

ANDERSON, ALEXANDER, born 1751, farmer in the Mains of Loggie, died 10 April 1819, husband of Elisabeth Forbes. [Migvie gravestone, Aberdeenshire]

ANDERSON, CHARLES, born 1751, farmer in Daugh, died 10 September 1806, father of Robert & Charles. [Migvie gravestone]

ANDERSON, DAVID, in Mill of Haugh, Strachan, Kincardineshire, testament, 23 November 1709, Comm. Brechin. [NRS]

ANDERSON, ELSPETH, relict of Alexander Scott schoolmaster at Birse, a deed, 4 May 1752. [NRS.RD3.211/2.227]

ANDERSON, JAMES, born 1720, son of David Anderson farmer at Bogiehill, Lintrathen, a Jacobite in 1745. [OR.11][LPR.196]

ANDERSON, JAMES, in Linrose, Airlie, a Jacobite in 1745. [OR.11]

ANDERSON, JOHN, in Auchrannie, Glen Isla, Angus, 1770. [NRS.E106.16.5]

ANDERSON, ROBERT, in Loanhead of Collow, Cortachy, Angus, testament, 1741, Comm. Brechin. [NRS]

ANDERSON, WILLIAM, in Charleston of Aboyne, Aberdeenshire, papers, 1751. [NRS.GD312.20]

ANDERSON, WILLIAM, born 1761, died at Tilligarmonth, Birse, 5 December 1851, husband of Janet Masson, born 17772, died 17 March 1852, parents of Alexander and William Anderson. [Kincardine O'Neil gravestone]

ANNANDALE, JOHN, tenant in Burnside, Lochlee, Angus, 1716. [NRS.E650.4]

ANNANDALE, THOMAS, tenant in Daughtie, Lochlee, Angus, 1716. [NRS.E650.4]

ARCHER, ANDREW, a herd in Blackston, Angus, husband of Agnes Fairweather born 1689, died 1735, parents of David, James, and Johanna. [Airlie gravestone]

ARCHIBALD, DAVID, in Glen Effock, Angus, father of William, Jean, and David, baptised at Lochlee, Angus, 1730s. [DUAS.BrMs.DC.3/174]

ARCHIBALD, JOHN, tenant in Tullidovie, Lethnot, Angus, 1716. [NRS.E650.4]

ARCHIBALD, WILLIAM, tenant in Glenifach, Lochlee, Angus, 1716. [NRS.E650.4]

ARMSTRONG, JOHN, drummer or piper of the 1st Strathspey Fencible Regiment, 1793. [NRS.GD248.463.1]

ARNOT, JAMES, born 1725, farmer at Bridgeton, Angus, died 1791. [Airlie gravestone]

BADENOCH, WILLIAM, minister of Cortachy, Angus, from 1725 to 1737. [F.5.281]

BAIN, ANDREW, in Glen Cluny, Angus, husband of Margaret Shaw, a sasine, 1718. [NRS.RS35.13.555]

BALFOUR, JAMES, born in Banchory-Ternan, Kincardineshire, in 1731, a missionary in Newfoundland from 1764 to his death there in 1792. [EMA.12][FPA.299/327][LIS.5.3]

BALFOUR, JOHN, tenant in Shelly, Lochlee, Angus, testament, 1799, Comm. Brechin. [NRS]

BALLENTYNE, THOMAS, in Kirkton of Glen Isla, Angus, a sasine, 1718. [NRS.RS35.13.476]

BANNERMAN, Sir ALEXANDER, of Elsiclk, land-owner of Glendye and Blackhall in the parish of Strachan, Kincardineshire, 1771. [NRS.E106.18.3]

BANNERMAN, MARY, was jointly granted a Crown Charter of the lands of Strachan, Kincardineshire, in 1775. [NRS.SIG1.21.34]

BARNET, JAMES, born 1705, son of John Barry, a workman in Kingoldrum, a Jacobite in 1745. [AOR.13]

BARRIE, WILLIAM, wife Ann Rood born 1708, died 1753. [Kingoldrum gravestone, Angus]

BAXTER, JOHN, born 1681, in Craigie Bridge, Angus, died 1749, husband of Isobel Black, born 1691, died 1751, parents of Andrew, and John. [Fern gravestone, Angus]

BEARN, ANDREW, wright at the Mill of Crovack, Angus, deed, 1719. [NRS.E615.10]

BEARN, ALEXANDER, and daughter Janet, in Clochie, Lethnott, Angus, 1725. [DUAS.Br.Ms.DC3.174]

BEATON, PATRICK, Corporal of the 1st Strathspey Fencible Regiment, 1793. [NRS.GD248.463.1]

BEATTIE, JOHN, a taxpayer in Netherton, Glenbucket, 1799. [ACA]

BEGG, GEORGE, born 1787, wood merchant at the Bridgend of Aboyne, died 31 March 1853, husband of Jean McLaggan, born 1805, died 4 April 1879. [Aboyne gravestone]

BEGG, JAMES, a taxpayer in Badinoan, Glenbucket, Aberdeenshire, 1799. [ACA]

BELL, DAVID, a farmer in Wellford, husband of Isobel Tindal who died in 1729, parents of John Bell. [Fern gravestone, Angus]

BELL, WILLIAM, a ploughman in Kinalty, Airlie, a Jacobite in 1745. [OR.13]

BELL, WILLIAM, born 1747, blacksmith to the Earl of Aboyne, died January 1823, husband of Margaret Masson, born 1764, died February 1849, parents of Isabel. [Aboyne gravestone]

BELLY, JAMES, died 1711, spouse to Isabel Stewart. [Edzell gravestone, Angus]

BERTIE, DAVID, miller at the Mill of Dalbog, father of Charles Bertie, born 1736, died 1757. [Edzell gravestone, Angus]

BERTIE, JAMES, in Craigindowy, Lethnot, Angus, 1752. [NRS.CH2.628.1.122]

BISHOP, JOHN, tenant in Slateford, Angus, husband of Janet Duncan, born 1694, died 1747. [Edzell gravestone, Angus]

BLACK, ALEXANDER, in Kirkton of Kingoldrum, Angus, testament, 1731, Comm. Brechin. [NRS]

BLACK, DAVID, born 1740, farmer in Barrelwell, Angus, died 1797, husband of Elizabeth Webster. [Fern gravestone, Angus]

BLACK, DAVID, born 1751, died 1806, spouse Janet White, born 1751, died 1825, parents of Elizabeth, John, George, and Alexander. [Strathcathro gravestone, Angus]

BLACK, JAMES, tenant of the Mill of Lethnot, Angus, 1716. [NRS.E650.4]

BLACK, JAMES, a tenant farmer at the Wood, Edzell, Angus, spouse Janet Wallas, born 1680, died 1745. [Lethnot gravestone, Angus]

BLACK, JAMES, in Dalbog, Lethnot, Angus, testament, 1751. [NRS.CH2.628.1]; born at the Mill of Lethnot, died at the Wood of Dalbog in 1750. [Lethnot gravestone]

BLACK, JANET, daughter of the late James Black at the Mill of Lethnot, Angus, testament, 1743, Comm. Brechin. [NRS]

BLACK, ROBERT, tenant in Clochie, Angus, spouse of Isabel Webster, born 1705, died 1743. [Lethnot gravestone]

BLAIR, DAVID, MA, minister at Lochlee, Angus, from 1729 to 1733. [F.5.401/501]

BLAIR, JOHN, elder of the parish of Cortachy and Clova, Angus, in 1748. [NRS.CH2.561.3.13]

BLAIR, WILLIAM, born 1727, son of Patrick Blair, a workman in Knowe of Kingoldrum, a Jacobite in 1745. [OR.14]

BOWES, MARGARET, in Lethnot, testament, 1792, Comm. Brechin. [NRS]

BOWMAN, ALEXANDER, in Milton of Glen Esk, Angus, testament, 1764, Comm. Brechin. [NRS]

BOWMAN, DAVID, tenant in Berriehill, Lochlee, Angus, 1716. [NRS.E650.4]

BOWMAN, DAVID, in Middlefoord, and daughter Janet, at Lochlee, Angus, 1735. [DUAS.BrMs.DC3.174]

SCOTTISH HIGHLANDERS, 1725-1775; GRAMPIAN HIGHLANDS, II

BOWMAN, JAMES, tenant in Lochlee, Angus, 1716. [NRS.E650.4]

BOWMAN, JAMES, in Easter Kinnordie, Angus, 1739. [NRS.GD205.Box 26/199]

BOWMAN, JOHN, schoolmaster in Glen Prosen, Angus, 1690. [SHS.4.2]

BOWMAN, JOHN, and daughter Agnes, at Achsallarie, Lochlee, Angus, 1733. [DUAS.BrMsDC3.174]

BOWMAN, THOMAS, in Drumcairn, Lethnot, Angus, 1725. [DUAS.BrMsDC3.174]

BOWMAN, WILLIAM, tenant in Berriehill, Lochlee, Angus, 1716. [NRS.E650.4]

BOWMAN, WILLIAM, born 1739, died 1807. [Crathie gravestone, Aberdeenshire]

BOWMAN, WILLIAM, tenant in Berriehill, Lochlee, 1716. [NRS.E650.4]

BOWMAN, WILLIAM, in Tirrybuckle, Lochlee, Angus, 1735. [DUAS.BrMsDC3.174]

BOWMAN, WILLIAM, born 1755, late in Bellendorie, Inchmarnoch, died 22 March 1821, husband of Margaret Small, born 1760, died 13 October 1827. [Glen Muick gravestone]

BRAND, WILLIAM, born 1752, tenant in Bogmore, died 22 February 1817, husband of Jean Ross, born 1765, died 9 September 1834. [Strachan gravestone, Kincardineshire]

BROUN, ALEXANDER, died in 1732. [Lochlee gravestone, Angus]

BROWN, ALEXANDER, and son John, in Milntown, Lochlee, Angus, 1731. [DUAS.BrMsDC3.174]

BROWN, ALEXANDER, and son Alexander, in Achronie, Lochlee, Angus, 1735. [DUAS.BrMsDC3.174]

BROWN, ALEXANDER, born 1755, died in Newton in 1803, husband of Mary Grant. [Strathcathro gravestone, Angus]

BROUN, ALEXANDER, died in 1732. [Lochlee gravestone, Angus]

BROWN, DONALD, in Rinechat, died aged 73, spouse Janet Shaw, born 1751, died 1836, parents of John and James Brown. [Crathie gravestone, Aberdeenshire]

BROWN, GEORGE, minister of Glen Muick, born 1750, died 24 July 1815, husband of (1) Elizabeth, born 1759, died 22 June 1795, (2) Ann Gordon, born 1760, died 1 February 1850. [Glen Muick gravestone]; a taxpayer in Glen Muick, 1799. [ACA]

BROWN, JAMES, schoolmaster in Cortachy, Angus, 1690. [SHS.4.2]

BROWN, JOHN, born 1770, died 9 April 1832, husband of Elisabeth Coutts, born 1773, died 25 January 1860. [Kincardine O'Neil gravestone]

BROWN, LAWRENCE, schoolmaster in Blair Atholl, Perthshire, 1699. [DPD.2.96]

BROWN, WILLIAM, at the Mill of Syde, Strathcathro, Angus, died 1711, testament, 1711, Comm. Brechin. [NRS]; husband of Jean Esplin, died 1703. [Strathcathro gravestone]

BROWN, WILLIAM, minister of Cortachy, Angus, from 1746 to 1748. [F.V.280]

BRUCE, ANDREW, MA, minister of Cortachy, Angus, from 1701 to 1705. [F.5.280]

BRUCE, JAMES, born 1666, tenant in Westside, died 1738, father of David, James, Isobel, John, Agnes, Margaret, Katherine, Jean, Robert, and Mary. [Edzell gravestone, Angus] [DUAS.BrMs.DC3.174]

BRUCE, WILLIAM, born 1750, farmer of Heughhead, died 18 February 1813. [Kincardine O'Neil gravestone]

BUCHAN, DAVID, a ploughman at the Milton of Glen Esk, a Jacobite in 1745. [OR.15]

BURGESS, BESSIE, only child of John Burgess in Achriagall, Strathspey, and his wife Christian Dallas, testament, 1744. [NRS.GD23.4.153]

BURNETT, ALEXANDER, born 1682, tenant in Upper Brathens, died 29 August 1730. [Banchory Ternan gravestone]

BURNETT, DAVID, born 1769, farmer in Goukstile, died 1841, husband of Ann Bain, born 1778, died 1865. [Birse gravestone, Aberdeenshire]

BURNET, JANET, born 1722, died 20 November 1797. [Banchory Ternan gravestone]

BURNETT, JOHN, born 1691, farmer in Drumfreny, died 1749, husband of Isabel Imray, born 1712, died 1791. [Banchory Ternan gravestone]

BURNETT, REBEKAH, born 1726, died 1789, spouse to James Watt a wright in Knows. [Birse gravestone, Aberdeenshire]

BUY, ALEXANDER, tenant in Castletoun, Lordship of Mar, Aberdeenshire, 1716. [NRS.E646.2.1]

CADGER, MARGARET, in Lethnot, Angus, 1758. [NRS.CH2.628.1.186]

CAIE, ROBERT, born 1697, farmer in Glassel, died 1770, husband of Elisabeth Meston, born 1712, died 1783, parents of Agnes, James, Alexander, and Mary. [Banchory-Ternan gravestone, Kincardineshire]

CAIRNCROSS, THOMAS, born 1683, farmer at Brone of Baldovie, died 1746. [Kincaldrum gravestone, Angus]

CAITHNESS, JAMES, born 1767, tenant of Duryhill, died 1830, husband of Jean Roberson, born 1774, died 1859. [Edzell gravestone, Angus]

CALDER, ISAAC, born 1756, farmer in Graystone, died 3 April 1845, husband of Margaret McConnach, born 1765, died 1796. [Glen Muick gravestone]; a taxpayer in Glen Muick, 1799. [ACA]

CALDER, ..., tenant in the wood of Ballachbouie, 1758. [NRS.GD30.73]

CALUM, THOMAS, a shoemaker in Grantown-on-Spey, Moray, 1769. [NRS.GD248.533.3.49]

CAMERON, JEAN, in Notwall, Cortachy and Clova, Angus, 1748. [NRS.CH2.561.3.13]

CAMPBELL, ALEXANDER, tenant in Castletoun, Lordship of Mar, Aberdeenshire, 1716. [NRS.E646.2.1/2]

CAMPBELL, ALEXANDER, of Corriecarmaig, tenant in Struan, a letter, 1755. [NRS.E783.9]

CAMPBELL, DAVID, a tenant in Ardoch, Lochlee, Angus, 1716. [NRS.E650.4]

CAMPBELL, DAVID, in Charlestown of Aboyne, a deed, 3 April 1752. [NRS.RD4/178/1.368]

CAMPBELL, JAMES, son of Reverend David Campbell, graduated MA from St Andrews in 1679, minister of Menmuir, Angus, from 1696 to 1700, died 1720. [F.5.408]

CAMPBELL, JAMES, a tenant in Dilbrach, Lochlee, Angus, 1716. [NRS.E650.4]

CANDOW, JOHN, a ploughman at Longdrum, Lintrathen, a Jacobite in 1745. [OR.16]

CARDEAN, DAVID, born 1708, tenant in Easter Denoon, died 1771, husband of Helen Malcolm, parents of Isobel and Helen, [Airlie gravestone, Angus]

CARGILL, JAMES, in Blackdykes of Incherick, Glen Isla, Angus, testament, 1783, Comm. Brechin. [NRS]

CARGILL, JOHN, a ploughman at Braidston, Airlie, a Jacobite in 1745. [OR.16]

CARGILL or WANLESS, JANET, born 1765, died 1826. [Glen Isla gravestone, Angus]

CARNEGIE, ALEXANDER, of Balnamoon, Angus, a Jacobite in 1715. [St AUL.Cheap ms5/537]

CARNEGIE, ANDREW, born 1641, in Moortoun, died 1714. [Fern gravestone, Angus]

CARNEGIE, JAMES, tenant in Brucklaw, Lethnot, Angus, 1716. [NRS.E650.4]

CARNEGIE, JAMES, the younger of Balnamoon, Menmuir, born 1713, eldest son of Alexander Carnegie, a Jacobite in 1745, died 1791. [P.2.100][OR.2]

CARNEGIE, JAMES, in Mergie, Edzell, Angus. testament, 1769, Comm. St Andrews. [NRS]

CARNEGIE, JOHN, in Coalmylie, Edzell, Angus, testament, 1769, Comm. St Andrews. [NRS]

CARNEGIE, JOHN, born 1768, tenant in Milton, died 1829, husband of Betty Duncan, born 1774, died 1865. [Lethnot gravestone, Angus]

CATANACH, ALEXANDER, born 1767, tenant of Bellwood, died 1853, husband of Lillie Ross, born 1767, died 1831. [Birse gravestone, Aberdeenshire]

CATTENACH, DONALD, in Braemar, Aberdeenshire, 1714. [NRS.GD124.15.1118.3]

CATTENACH, JOHN, a servant of William Ogilvy in Meikle Kenny, Kingoldrum, a Jacobite in 1745. [OR.16]

CATTENACH, JOHN, a taxpayer in Kinloch, Crathie, 1799. [ACA]

CATTENACH, SHAW, born 1752, died 20 April 1842, husband of Jean Birss, born 1754, died 28 October 1809, in Forest of Birse, son Alexander, born 1800, died October 1836. [Birse gravestone]

CHALMERS, ALEXANDER, factor of Hugh Rose of Clova, Angus, 1762. [NRS.CS214,66]

CHAPLAIN, JAMES, a workman in Arnboggie, Lintrathen, a Jacobite in 1745. [OR.17]

CHAPMAN, WILLIAM, from Cullen of Aboyne, Aberdeenshire, once a shoemaker in Glasgow, later a soldier of the 3rd Foot Guards Regiment, married Menny Catherine Stewart, daughter of Andrew Stewart a feuar in Blair Drummond, Stirlingshire, in July 1782, a process of divorce in December 1788. [NRS.CC8.6.796]

CHISHOLM, JOHN, Sergeant of the 1st Strathspey Fencible Regiment, 1793. [NRS.GD248.463.1]

CHREE, WILLIAM, a taxpayer in Milltown, Glenbucket, 1799. [ACA]

CHRISTIE, CHARLES, born 1736, tenant in Cowiehill, died 1788, husband of Jane Brake, born 1728, died 1812. [Edzell gravestone, Angus]

CHRISTIE, DAVID, born 1682, tenant in Dalbog, died 1758, husband of Helen Gordon, born 1709, died 1764. [Edzell gravestone, Angus]

CHRISTIE, PETER, a ploughman in Lindertis, Airlie, a Jacobite in 1745. [OR.17]

CHRISTIE, PETER, born 1734, tenant in Dalbog, died 1780. [Edzell gravestone, Angus]

CHRISTIE, WILLIAM, in Bachentaich, Crathie, Aberdeenshire, a bankrupt in 1768. [NRS.GD248.533.2.63]

CHRISTISON, ALEXANDER, tenant in Auchronnie, Lochlee, Angus, 1716. [NRS.E650.4]

CHRISTISON, DAVID, tenant in Corhairnros, Lochlee, Angus, 1716. [NRS.E650.4]

CHRISTISON, DAVID, tenant in Bellie, Lochlee, Angus, 1716. [NRS.E650.4]

CHRISTISON, DAVID, born 1685, died 1743, husband of Jean Adam, born 1695, died 1742, parents of Jean, Alexander, and John. [Edzell gravestone, Angus]

SCOTTISH HIGHLANDERS, 1725-1775; GRAMPIAN HIGHLANDS, II

CHRISTISON, DAVID, born 1700, tenant farmer in Auchronie, died 1761, husband of Helen Mills or Milne, born 1711, died 1775. [Lochlee gravestone, Angus]

CHRISTISON, JAMES, tenant in Midtoun, Lochlee, Angus, 1716. [NRS.E650.4]

CHRISTISON, JAMES, in Whiggonton, Glen Esk, Angus, testament, 1793, Comm. Brechin. [NRS]

CHRISTISON, JOHN, tenant in Couroror, Lochlee, Angus, 1716. [NRS.E650.4]

CHRISTISON, ROBERT, tenant in Glack, Lochlee, Angus, 1716. [NRS.E650.4]

CHRISTISON, THOMAS, tenant in Auchronie, Lochlee, Angus, 1716. [NRS.E650.4]

CHRISTISON, THOMAS, tenant in Weste Achrony, Lochlee, Angus, died in 1744. [Lochlee gravestone, Angus]

CLARK, ALEXANDER, a workman on the Braes of Auldallan, Lintrathen, a Jacobite in 1745. [OR.17]

CLARK, DAVID, and his wife Elizabeth Taylor, in Lethnot, Angus, 1764. [NRS.CH2.628.1.251]

CLARK, JAMES, servant to James Wright in Berie, Lintrathen, a Jacobite in 1745. [OR.18]

CLARK, JAMES, in Weetlands, Glen Isla, Angus, 1770. [NRS.E106.16.5]

CLERK, JOHN, tenant in Droustie, Lochlee, Angus, 1716. [NRS.E650.4]

CLARK, MALCOLM, born 1758, farmer in Balmore, Aberdeenshire, died 1845, spouse Janet McGregor died 1803. [Braemar gravestone, Aberdeenshire]

CLARK, Mrs, a taxpayer in Crathie, 1799. [ACA]

CLEPHAN, THOMAS, minister in Kingoldrum, Angus, testament, 1717, Comm. Brechin. [NRS]

CLOUDSLY, DAVID, born 1778, died 6 September 1823, husband of Mary Glenny, born 1789, died 9 October 1865. [Banchory Ternan gravestone]

CLUNIE, JOHN, in Whine, Cortachy, Angus, husband of Rachel Reoch testament, 1783, Comm. Brechin. [NRS]

COBB, JOHN, in the parish of Navar, Angus, 1726. [NRS.CH2.628.17]

CONDIE, WILLIAM, a schoolmaster at Faulds of Derry, Glen Isla, Angus, 1755. [SSPCK#18]

CONSTABLE, or GLENDY, AGNES, born 1674, died 1732, mother of Andrew Glendy. [Airlie gravestone, Angus]

CONSTABLE, JOHN, minister at Kingoldrum, Angus, and spouse Magdalene Ogilvie, testaments, 1704 and 1707, Comm. Brechin. [NRS]

COOPER, GEORGE, born 1749, a merchant in Slateford, died 1831, husband of Jean Lindsay, born 1751, died 1841, parents of George, Margaret, David, Mary, and James. [Edzell gravestone, Angus]

COPINS, DAVID, a workman in Barnton, Kingoldrum, a Jacobite in 1745. [OR.18]

COSSINS, JOHN, and his wife Janet Spalding, in Knapieley, Clova, testament, 1742, Comm. Brechin. [NRS]

COUPAR, JOHN, a tenant in the Mill of Glassrosie, Lethnot, Angus, 1716. [NRS.E650.4]

COUTTS, ALEXANDER, in Ballachbuie, testament, 1727, Comm. Aberdeen. [NRS]

COUTTS, ALEXANDER, tenant in Bellachlon, Lordship of Mar, Aberdeenshire, 1716. [NRS.E646.2.1]

COUTTS, GEORGE, in Monaltry, born 1743, died 1814, spouse May Maxwel, born 1752, died 1795. [Crathie gravestone, Aberdeenshire]

COUTTS, GEORGE, born 1730, farmer in the Mill of Campfied, died 5 January 1798, husband of Jean Spence, born 1730, died 1808. [Kincardine O'Neil gravestone, Aberdeenshire]

COUTS, JAMES, SPCK schoolmaster at the Braes of Cromar 1726-1727. [SRS.20.19]

COUTTS, JAMES, son of William Coutts a weaver in Glen Muick, was apprenticed to Alexander Lichton a weaver for 8 years, 1719. [ACA]

COUTTS, JOHN, a tenant in Glentenant, Lethnot, Angus, 1716. [NRS.E650.4]

COUTTS, JOHN, tenant in Bellachlon, Lordship of Mar, Aberdeenshire, 1716. [NRS.E646.2.1]

COUTTS, JOHN, in Lochlee, Angus, testament, 1741, Comm. Brechin. [NRS]

COUTTS, JOHN, in the parish of Kindrochit, Lordship of Mar, Aberdeenshire, 1716. [NRS.E646.2.2]

COUTTS, JOHN, born 1761, died 1833. [Glenmuick gavestone]

COUTS, PETER, a merchant in Balmoral, 1732; a contract to build a sawmill on the Water of Tanner near the Haughs of Allachie in1732. [NRS.GD181.191/12; 198/2]

COUTS, ROBERT, born 1703, died 3 July 1732, son of Thomas Couts a shoemaker in Lochtoun of Leys. [Banchory-Ternan gravestone]

CRAFTS, DAVID, schoolmaster in Inverarity and Fearn, Angus, 1690. [SHS.4.2]

CRAICK, JOHN, born 1669, farmer at Brea of Old Allan, died 1740, spouse Margaret Davidsn, parents of James. [Lintrathen gravestone, Angus]

CRAIG, THOMAS, a tenant in Tarbracks, Glen Ogilvie, Angus, an inhibition, 1784. [NRS.D1.128.1.xlvii.460]

CRAIK, DAVID, in Nether Scythie, Lintrathen, a Jacobite in 1745. [OR.19]

CRAIK, JAMES, in Craik, Kinnordy, Angus, 1755. [NRS.GD205.29.239]

CRAIK, JOHN, in Upper Scythie, Lintrathen, a Jacobite in 1745. [OR.19]

CRAMOND, ISOBEL, relict of Frederick Lyon minister at Airlie, a bond, 1716, assigned to Captain William Cramond of Ardblair in 1718, and later by his son and heir William Cramond of Ardblair. [NRS.GD16.42.692]

CRICHTON, DAVID, in Caldhame, Clova, Angus, husband of Margaret Shirrell, testament, 1700, Comm. Brechin. [NRS]

CRICHTON, JOHN, servant to Thomas Adam of Cheatley, Lintrathen, a Jacobite in 1745. [OR.19]

CRICHTON, THOMAS, in Brulzeon, Lintrathen, a Jacobite in 1745. [OR.19]

CROCKET, DAVID, a tenant in Migvie, Lochlee, Angus, 1716. [NRS.E650.4]

CROCKET, HENRY, a tenant in Kisme, Lochlee, Angus, 1716. [NRS.E650.4]

CROCKET, JAMES, a workman in Kingoldrum, a Jacobite in 1745. [OR.20]

CROCKET, JOHN, in Glenesk, a tenant in Lochlee, Angus, 1716. [NRS.E650.4]

CROCKET, MARGARET, in Lethnot, Angus, 1752. [NRS.CH2.628.1.88]

CROCKET, WILLIAM, a tenant in Tarfside, Lochlee, Angus, 1716. [NRS.E650.4]

CROCKET, WILLIAM, in Lethnot, Angus, 1716. [NRS.CH2.628.1.153]

CROMAR, GEORGE, born 1664, died 1730, husband of Jean Turner, born 1676, died 1739. [Birse gravestone, Aberdeenshire]

CROMAR, GEORGE, MA, born 1777, schoolmaster at Bankhead of Birse, died 1829, husband of Margaret Barclay, born 1780, died 1862. [Banchory Ternan gravestone, Kincardineshire]

CROMAR, JEAN, born 1693, spouse to James Rose in Kirktown of Birse, died 1756. [Birse gravestone, Aberdeenshire]

CROMAR, PETER, a taxpayer in Leyhead, Glen Muick, 1799. [ACA]

CRUICKSHANK, GEORGE, an advocate, was served heir to his grandfather Robert Cruickshank of Banchory, Aberdeenshire, in 1724. [NRS.S/H]

CRUICKSHANK, PATRICK, of Strathcathro, Angus, 1792. [NRS.RHP83]

CRUICKSHANK, ROBERT, was granted the lands of Banchory, Aberdeenshire, in 1724. [NRS.SIG1.30.58]; family papers, 1705-1743. [NRS.GD7.1.60]; heritor of the salmon fishing on the Dee, 1708. [ACA.APB.2]

CUMMIN, DUNCAN, a taxpayer in Castleton, Crathie, 1799. [ACA]

CUMMIN, WILLIAM, a taxpayer in Auchindrine, Crathie, 1799. [ACA]

CUMMING, ALEXANDER, SSPCK at New Perk, Tullich, 1792-1813. [SRS.20.20]

CUMING, CHARLES, in Tarland, Aberdeenshire, testament, 1799, Comm. Aberdeen. [NRS]

CUMING, DAVID, procurator fiscal of the baron court of Strathspey, 1764-1768. [NRS.GD248.437.7]

CUMMING, DUNCAN, drummer or piper of the 1st Strathspey Fencible Regiment, 1793. [NRS.GD248.463.1]

CUTHBERT, ARCHIBALD, a ploughman in Balnamoon, Menmuir, Angus, a Jacobite in 1745. [OR.20]

DANSKIN, JAMES, in Nether Migby, Kinnordy, Angus, 1755. [NRS.GD205.29.239]

DARGY, MARGARET, in Lethnot, Angus, 1758. [NRS.CH2.628.1.177]

DAUNEY, WILLIAM, son of William Dauney in Finnylost, parish of Strathdon, was apprenticed to James Dauney a shoemaker in Aberdeen, for 5 years, 19 June 1788. Cautioner was William McCook in Colquharrie, in the parish of Strathdon. [ACA]

DAVIDSON, ALEXANDER, in Lethnot, Angus, 1769. [NRS.CH2.628.1.260]

DAVIDSON, ALEXANDER, a taxpayer in Inver Mill, Crathie, 1799. [ACA]

DAVIDSON, BARBARA, born 1765, died 10 August 1805. [Kincardine O'Neil gravestone]

DAVIDSON, CHARLES, of Midmar, Aberdeenshire, testament, 1777, Comm. Aberdeen. [NRS]

DAVIDSON, DUNCAN, Corporal of the 1st Strathspey Fencible Regiment, 1793. [NRS.GD248.463.1]

DAVIDSON, GEORGE, born 1745, a student, died 1760. [Lethnot gravestone, Angus]

DAVIDSON, JOHN, born 1775, son of David Davidson farmer in Pitready, died 11 December 1802. [Strachan gravestone]

DAVIDSON, PETER, born 1737, late in Ballandory, died 11 February 1806, husband of Elizabeth Duncan, born 1746, died 12 November 1788. [Glen Muick gravestone]

DAVIDSON, WILLIAM, a tenant in Migvie, Lochlee, 1716. [NRS.E650.4]

DAVIDSON, WILLIAM, born 1702, graduated MA from Marischal College, Aberdeen, in 1728, schoolmaster of Navar, Angus, minister of Lethnot from 1746 to his death in 1775, test., 1775, Comm. Brechin; husband of Janet Farroes, parents of George, and Alexander. [F.5.399]

DAVIDSON, WILLIAM, born 1776, farmer in Balfour, died 1861, husband of Helen Begg, born 1777, died 1846. [Birse gravestone, Aberdeenshire]

DAVIE, JOHN, minister at Strathcathro and factor to the Earl of Southesk, a Jacobite, deposed in 1716. [F.3.418][NRS.CH2.575.1]

DAVIE, JOHN, in Newmilne of Birse, Aberdeenshire, testament, 1794, Comm. Aberdeen. [NRS]

DAVIE, JOHN, tenant in the Brae of Airlie, Angus, and Elizabeth McLaren, daughter of the deceased David McLaren in Buchall, a marriage contract, 1798. [NRS.GD15.44.46]

DAVIE, WILLIAM, in Brae of Airlie, Angus, 1732. [NRS.GD16.Sec.28.339]

DAWSON, JAMES, a taxpayer in Balnacraig, Glenbucket, 1799. [ACA]

DEAVIE, JOHN, born 1712, died 1732. [Birse gravestone, Aberdeenshire]

DENNIE, JOHN, born 1772, farmer at Bogieshiel, died 1 November 1845, husband of Ann Ross, born 8 June 1784, died 12 August 1872. [Birse gravestone]

DENS, JOHN, husband of Isabel Macher, born 1675, died 1713. [Lintrathen gravestone, Angus]

DEUCHARS, JOHN, hammerman in Burnside of Kinclune, Angus, husband of Janet Candow, died 1721, parents of John and Robert. [Lintrathen gravestone, Angus]

DEUCHARS, JOHN, ploughman in Glen Ogilvy, a Jacobite in 1745. [OR.21]

DICKSON, THOMAS, born 1730, tenant in Cossacks, died 1802, husband of Jean Low, parents of William, David, and John. [Cortachy gravestone, Angus]

DICK, JOHN, born 1684, a farmer in Over Ascreavie, died 1767, husband of Margaret Bunch, born 1682, died 1748. [Kingoldrum gravestone, Angus]

SCOTTISH HIGHLANDERS, 1725-1775; GRAMPIAN HIGHLANDS, II

DICKSON, THOMAS, born 1730, tenant in Cossacks, died 1802, husband of Jean Low, parents of William, David, and John. [Cortachy gravestone, Angus]

DINGWALL, ALEXANDER, in Knockgranish, Strathspey, papers, 1783-1794. [NRS.GD248.498.4-5]

DINGWALL, JOHN, Corporal of the 1st Strathspey Fencible Regiment, 1793. [NRS.GD248.463.1]

DINGWALL, MARY, only daughter of Donald Dingwall, deceased, tenant in Dell of Granish, Strathspey, papers, 1793. [NRS.GD248.498.4-5]

DINNIE, ROBERT, born 1766, famer in Alancreich, died 1847. [Birse gravestone]

DOCTOR, PETER, born 1722, son of Patrick Doctor, a ploughman in Glen Ogilvy, a Jacobite in 1745. [OR.21]

DOIG, DAVID, of Nether Migby, Kinnordy, Angus, 1755. [NRS.GD205.29.239]

DOIG, JOHN, session clerk of the parish of Cortachy and Clova, Angus, 1748. [NRS.CH2.561.3.13]

DON, ALEXANDER, born 1746, in Ballownie, died 1808. [Strathcathro gravestone. Angus]

DONALD, JAMES, in Glen Isla, a Jacobite in 1746. [P.2.146]

DONALD, JAMES, schoolmaster in Clova and Glen Prosen, Angus, 1749 to 1758. [SSPCK#23]

DONALD, JOHN, tenant in Ednaughty, born 1683, died 1745, husband of Jean Ogilvie, [Glen Prosen gravestone, Angus]

DONALD, JOHN, servant to Alexander Farquharson in Inzion, Lintrathen, a Jacobite in 1745. [OR.21]

DONALDSON, JAMES, a tenant in Arsellach, Lochlee, Angus, 1716. [NRS.E650.4]

DOROE, JOHN, in Dilwhiper, died 1712. [Edzell gravestone, Angus]

DOUGLAS, JAMES, minister of Aboyne and Glentanar, Aberdeenshire, 1700-1715. [F.6.78]

DOUGLAS, JOHN, land-owner of Gellan in the parish of Strachan, Kincardineshire, 1771. [NRS.E106.18.3]

DOUGLASS, ROBERT, born 1763, farmer in North Nook, died 11 June 1821, husband of Ann Grieg, born 1764, died 28 December 1837. [Banchory Ternan gravestone]

DOWNIE, DAVID, portioner of Inverquharity, Angus, an inhibition, 1792. [NRS.D1.128.1.xxviii.165]

DOWNIE, JAMES, a taxpayer in Crathie, Aberdeenshire, 1799. [ACA]

DOWNIE, JOHN, SSPCK schoolmaster in Folda, Glenisla, from 1756 to 1759. [SRS.20.24]

DOWNIE, MARY, in Mosstown of the Braes of Cromar, a petition, 1783. [NRS.GD181.224/25]

DOWNIE, EBENEZER, ploughman in Blackhill, Airlie, a Jacobite in 1715. [OR.21]

DOUNIE, THOMAS, farmer in Gobertoun, Glen Isla, Angus, husband of Margaret Paton, born 1715, died 1748. [Glen Isla gravestone, Angus]

DOWNIE, THOMAS, portioner of Wester Inverquharrity, Angus, and Marjory Bressach, a marriage contract, 1789, West Milne of Glen Isla. [NRS.GD16.44.44]

DOWNIE, ..., spouse Elspet Coutts born 1720, died 1782, parents of James Downie born 1748, tenant in Crathenaird, Aberdeenshire, died 1819, of John Downie born 1750, died 1775. [Crathie gravestone, Aberdeenshire]

DUFF, WILLIAM, of Fetteresso, Kincardineshire, a tack, 1800. [NRS.GD105.557]

DUKE, JOHN, in Tilliegloom, Dunlappie and Strathcathro, Angus, testament, 1747, Comm. Brechin. [NRS]

DULLANACH, JOHN, a tenant in Bridge of Lee, Lochlee, Angus,1716. [NRS.E650.4]

DUNBAR, JOHN, educated at Marischal College, Aberdeen, minister of Menmuir, Angus, from 1709 to his death in 1744, husband of Elizabeth Ogilvie, parents of Margaret, Elizabeth, Katherine, Anne, John, Robert, and David. [F.5.408]

DUNBAR, ..., schoolmaster in Lethnot and Navar, Angus, 1747. [NRS.CH2.628.17]

DUNCAN, ALEXANDER, a tenant at Bridge of Lee, Lochlee, Angus, 1716. [NRS.E650.4]

DUNCAN, ALEXANDER, born 1700, schoolmaster, died 1763, husband of Ann Buchan, born 1714, died 1777. [Strathcathro gravestone, Angus]

DUNCAN, ALEXANDER, born 1777, farmer of the Mains of Findrack, died 4 September 1841, husband of Elizabeth Davie, born 1770, died 10 December 1853. [Kincardine O'Neil gravestone]

DUNCAN, CHARLES, in Lethnot, Angus, 1752. [NRS.CH2.628.1.110]

DUNCAN, DAVID, in Nether Drumhead, husband of Janet Craik, parents of Thomas, born 1711, died 1736, Lilias, and George. [Lintrathen gravestone, Angus]

DUNCAN, DAVID, born 1761, in Leybank of Kincardine O'Neil, died 3 May 1845, husband of Rachel Leighton, born 1772, died 1 March 1855. [Banchory Ternan gravestone]

DUNCAN, JAMES, of Wardhouse, born 1717, died 1792, husband of Jean Michie, born 1762, died 1795. [Edzell gravestone, Angus]

DUNCAN, JAMES, and his wife Isobel Robie, in the Kirkton of Clova, a sasine, 1725. [NRS.RS14,16]

DUNCAN, JOHN, servant to Thomas Hanton in Easter Coull, Lintrathen, a Jacobite in 1745. [OR.22]

DUNCAN, JOHN, born 1751, farmer in Runtaleave, died 1806, husband of Margaret Lindsay, born 1766, died 1844, parents of Charles, born 1793, died 1816. [Cortachy gravestone, Angus]

DUNCAN, JOHN, a farmer in Cormure, husband of May Gall, parents of William, born 1739, died 1771, also Charles, Isobel, Ranald, John, James, Frederick, Martha, Betty, and Samuel. [Glen Prosen gravestone, Angus]

DUNCAN, JOHN, born 1766, farmer in Broadgreens, died 6 March 1823, husband of Elspet Duthie, born 1761, died 4 July 1841. [Banchory Devenick gravestone, Aberdeenshire]

DUNCAN, PETER, born 1761, farmer in Oldyleiper, died 1831, husband of Jane Howie, born 1767, died 1840. [Birse gravestone, Aberdeenshire]

DUNCAN, PETER, a taxpayer in Tinnabach, Crathie, 1799. [ACA]

DUNCAN, ROBERT, in Braedounie, Clova, Angus, testament, 1718, Comm. Brechin. [NRS]

DUNCAN, ROBERT, farmer at the Milton of Glen Esk, a Jacobite in 1745. [OR.22]

DUNCAN, ROBERT, born 1740 in Rhynie, Aberdeenshie, a laborer, enlisted in the Aberdeenshire Fencibles in 1778. [NRS.GD44.47.11]

DUNCAN, ROBERT, born 1731, died 1804. [Crathie gravestone, Aberdeenshire]

DUNCAN, THOMAS, in Easter Loanhead, Glen Isla, Angus, 1770. [NRS.E106.16.5]

DUNCAN, WILLIAM, born 1734, farmer in Dalvorar, died 1792, father of Peter Duncan, born 1764, farmer in Tynabaich, died 1826. [Crathie gravestone, Aberdeenshire]

DURAY, JAMES, born 1709, son of John Duray of that Ilk, died 1743. [Edzell gravestone, Angus]

DURIE, ALEXANDER, in Slateford, Edzell, Angus, testament, 1777, Comm. St Andrews. [NRS]

DURIE, DAVID, of Duryhill, Angus, testament, 1751, Comm. St Andrews. [NRS]

DURIE, JOHN, of Duriehill, Edzell, Angus, relict Euphemia Lyell, testament, 1768, Comm. St Andrews. [NRS]

DURRO, JOHN, a tenant in Ardgoith, Lethnot, Angus, 1716. [NRS.E650.4]

DURWARD, ALEXANDER, born 1765, died 21 September 1838, husband of Margaret Begg, born 1774, died 21 November 1841. [Birse gravestone]

DURWARD, JAMES, born 1757, farmer in Pitreddie, Strachan, died 7 March 1817, husband of Isabella Ogg born 1759, died 12 January 1835, parents of Isobel, Frances, and Robert. [Birse gravestone]

DUTHIE, ALEXANDER, bon 1763, died 8 October 1823, husband of Christian Jameson. [Banchory Devenick gravestone, Aberdeenshire]

DUTHIE, JOHN, ploughman at Newton of Airlie, a Jacobite in 1745. [OR.22]

DUTHIE, JOHN, at the Mill of Glescarrie, Lethnot, Angus, testament, 1748, Comm. Brechin. [NRS]

EASSIE, JOHN, a labourer in Braidstone, Airlie, a Jacobite in 1745. [OR.23]

EDWARD, AGNES, in Piper Balgray, Kingoldrum, Angus, testament, 1715, Comm. Brechin. [NRS]

EDWARD, ALEXANDER, in Wester Persie, died 1727, husband of Isobel Ogilvy. [Kingoldrum gravestone, Angus]

EDWARD, ALEXANDER, in Easter Persie, later in Newbigging, Kingoldrum, testament, 1731, Comm. Brechin. [NRS]

EDWARD, ALEXANDER, a labourer in Hillockhead, Lintrathen, a Jacobite in 1745. [OR.23]

EDWARD, ALEXANDER, workman in Kingoldrum, a Jacobite in 1745. [OR.23][LPR.208]

EDWARD, ANDREW, born 25 April 1722, son of Alexander Edward in Kirriemuir, servant to William Grewar in Purgavie, Lintrathen, a Jacobite in 1745, transported to the West Indies in 1747. [OR.23][P.2.176][TNA.SP36.102]

EDWARD, ANDREW, workman in Newbigging, Lintrathen, a Jacobite in 1745. [OR.23]

EDWARD, ANDREW, a chapman in the Braes of Lintrathen, a Jacobite in 1745. [OR.2]

EDWARD, ELSPET, a widow in Glen Prosen, Angus, testament, Comm. St Andrews. [NRS]

EDWARD, JAMES, son of Alexander Edward in West Reverney, Lintrathen, a Jacobite in 1745, transported to the colonies in 1747. [OR.23][P.2.176]

EDWARD, JOHN, a tenant in Bellie, Lochlee, Angus, 1716. [NRS.E650.4]

EDWARD, JOHN, in Nether Sheithens, husband of Elisabeth Sharp, born 1677, died 1713. [Lintrathen gravestone, Angus]

EDWARD, JOHN, of Pearcies, Angus, testament, 1724, Comm. Brechin. [NRS]

EDWARD, JOHN, farmer in Kinclun, husband of Elspeth Hepburn, born 1689, died 1748. [Kingoldrum gravestone, Angus]

EDWARD, JOHN, a farmer in Needs, Lintrathen, a Jacobite in 1745. [OR.24]

EDWARD, JOHN, a workman in Bottom, Lintrathen, a Jacobite in 1745. [OR.24]

EDWARD, JOHN, in Greenlamirth, Lintrathen, a Jacobite in 1745. [OR.24]

EDWARD, JOHN, a Glen Isla a Jacobite in 1745. [P.2.176]

EDWARD, JOHN, the elder, in Wester Pearsie, Kingoldrum, Angus, testament, 1781, Comm. Brechin. [NRS]

ELDER, ROBERT, a tenant in Nether Cairncross, Lochlee, Angus, 1716. [NRS.E650.4]

ELLIS, ALEXANDER, labourer in Glen Ogilvy, a Jacobite in 1745. [OR.24]

ELLIS, JOHN, a labourer in Cardean, Airlie, a Jacobite in 1745. [OR.24]

ELMSLIE, ALEXANDER, born 1769, farmer in Cuttleburn, died 10 July 1840, husband of Jean Simpson, born 1771, died 28 January 1855. [Coull gravestone]

ELMSLIE, CHARLES, born 1743, farmer in Cove, died 26 November 1819, husband of Margaret Bruce, born 1751, died 12 April 1821. [Banchory Devenick gravestone]

ELMSLIE, JOHN, born 1776, in Colmuir, Coull, died 13 December 1850, husband of Helen Robbie, born 1781, died 10 March 1832. [Coull gravestone]

ELPHINSTONE, JOHN, of Bellabeg, and his children Alexander, James, and Elizabeth, a sasine re Tarland, Aberdeenshire, 1798. [NRS.GD33.52.9]

ERSKINE, ALEXANDER, in the parish of Kindrochit, Lordship of Mar, Aberdeenshire, 1716. [NRS.E646.2.2]

ERSKINE, DONALD, portioner of Achalader, lands of Crathie in the Lordship of Mar, Aberdeenshire, 1716. [NRS.E646.2.1]

ERSKINE, DONALD, in Westermicras, Tullich, Lordship of Mar, Aberdeenshire, 1716. [NRS.E646.2.1]

ERSKINE, GEORGE, tenant in Woodside of Edzell, Angus, an inhibition, 1782. [NRS.D1.128.1.xlvii.398]

ERSKINE, GREGOR, portioner of Achalader, lands of Crathie in the Lordship of Mar, Aberdeenshire, 1716. [NRS.E646.2.1]

EWAN, CHARLES, born 1790, of Waterside, died 22 February 1828, husband of Jean Smith, born 1792, died 9 July 1869. [Kincardine O'Neil gravestone]

EWAN, GEORGE, son of John Ewan in Greencots, Aboyne, a Jacobite in 1715. [JAB205]

EWAN, WILLIAM, son of John Ewan in Greencots, Aboyne, a Jacobite in 1715. [JAB.205]

EWART, JEAN, only daughter of William Ewart tenant in Inverquiech, and William Brown a wright in Alyth, eldest son and heir of David Brown a farmer in Rangend of Ruthven, a marriage contract, 1790. [NRS.GD15.45]

EWING, JAMES, a tenant in Eaglestoun of Glentenant, Lochlee, Angus, 1716. [NRS.E650.4]

FAIRWEATHER, ALEXANDER, tenant in Blairno, Navar, Angus, around 1726, died 1741, husband of Jean Mitchell. [NRS.CH2.628.17]

FAIRWEATHER, ANDREW, in Cadham, Kinnordy, Angus, 1755. [NRS.GD205.29.239]

FAIRWEATHER, GEORGE, in Braiko, Navar, Agus, testament, 1741, Comm. Brechin. [NRS]

FAIRWEATHER, JOHN, an apprentice to John Fairweather a tailor in Lethnot, Angus, 1758. [NRS.CH2.628.1.173]

FALCONER, ALEXANDER, son of John Falconer in Ashintilly, parish of Durris, was apprenticed to William Law a baker in Aberdeen, for 5 years, 5 December 1781. [ACA]

FALCONER, WILLIAM, Corporal of the 1st Strathspey Fencible Regiment, 1793. [NRS.GD248.463.1

FARQUHAR, DAVID, a labourer in Lindertis, Angus, a Jacobite in 1745. [OR.24]

FARQUHAR, WILLIAM, son of Robert Farquhar master of Banchory Grammar School, was apprenticed to William Smith, a merchant in Aberdeen, for 3 years, in 1711. [ACA]

SCOTTISH HIGHLANDERS, 1725-1775; GRAMPIAN HIGHLANDS, II

FARQUHARSON, ALEXANDER, of Monaltrie, Glencairn, Lordship of Mar, Aberdeenshire, 1716. [NRS.E646.2.1/2]

FARQUHARSON, ALEXANDER, the younger, son of Lewis Farquharson of Auchendryne, a Jacobite in 1715, died 1727, testament, 1727, Comm. Aberdeen. [NRS]

FARQUHARSON, ALEXANDER, a farmer at Inzeon, Lintrathen, a Jacobite in 1745. [OR.4]

FARQUHARSON, ALEXANDER, a miller at Inzion and Pitmudie, Aberdeenshire, dead by 1779, father of Susanna. [NRS.GD16.Sec.28.376]

FARQUHARSON, ALEXANDER, a workman in Easter Reverney, Lintrathen, a Jacobite in 1745. [OR.45]

FARQUHARSON, ALEXANDER, of Inverey, died at Balmoral in 1782, son of Lewis Farquharson of Auchindryne. [Braemar gravestone, Aberdeenshire]

FARQUHARSON, ALEXANDER, factor of the lands of Aboyne, 1764-1765. [NRS.GD181.202/156/10-12]

FARQUHARSON, CHARLES, of Balmoral, a Jacobite at the Battle of Killiecrankie in 1689, later in France, died 1747. [JAB.66]

FARQUHARSON, CHARLES, son of John Farquharson of Inverey, and Margaret Gordon, a Writer to the Signet, a Jacobite in 1715, died 1747. [JAB.63]

FARQUHARSON, CHARLES, a Roman Catholic priest in Braemar, died at Oirdearg in 1799, son of Lewis Farquharson of Auchindryne. [Braemar gravestone, Aberdeenshire]

FARQUHARSON, DAVID, of Richolly, Glencairn, Lordship of Mar, Aberdeenshire, 1716. [NRS.E646.2.1]

FARQUHARSON, DONALD, of Micras, Glen Muick, a Jacobite, fought t the Siege of Preston in 1715. [JAB.72][CRA.63]

FARQUHARSON, DONALD, of Camanasheift, lands of Kindrocht in the Lordship of Mar, Aberdeenshire, 1716. [NRS.E646.2.1]

FARQUHARSON, DONALD, in Easter Micras, Tullich, Lordship of Mar, Aberdeenshire, 1716. [NRS.E646.2.1]

FARQUHARSON, DONALD, of Coldrach, a Jacobite in 1715, acobite, fought at the Siege of Preston in 1715, died after 1733. [JAB.72]

FARQUHARSON, FRANCIS, of Finzean, was served heir to his father Francis Farquharson of Finzean, on 6 March 1711. [NRS.S/H]

FARQUHARSON, FRANCIS, a Jacobite in 1715, fought at the Siege of Preston in 1715, died in 1733. [JAB.70][CRA.43][CS.V.162]

FARQUHARSON, FRANCIS, of Monaltry, Aberdeenshire, 1747. [NRS.E773]

FARQUHARSON, FRAS., a taxpayer in White House, Glen Muick, 1799. [ACA]

FARQUHARSON, JAMES, of Tullochcowty, parish of Crathie, Lordship of Mar, 1716. [NRS.E646.2.2]

FARQUHARSON, JAMES, of Balmoral, a Jacobite in 1715, died in 1753. [JAB.65][CRA.60]

FARQUHARSON, JAMES, son of a farmer in Westerton of Lintrathen, Angus, a Jacobite in 1745. [OR.25]

FARQUHARSON, JAMES, a taxpayer in Invercauld, Crathie, 1799. [ACA]

FARQUHARSON, JAMES, in Balmoral, Glencairn, Lordship of Mar, Aberdeenshire, 1716. [NRS.E646.2.1/2]

FARQUHARSON, JAMES, of Tullochoy, deceased, Glencairn, Lordship of Mar, Aberdeenshire, 1716. [NRS.E646.2.1]

FARQUHARSON, JAMES, of Tullelnacoy, died 1760, spouse May Farquharson, died 1729. [Crathie gravestone, Aberdeenshire]

FARQUHARSON, JAMES, in Belnabodach, father of James Farquharson died 1805, Katherine died 1807, also Ann born 1808, died 1842. [Crathie gravestone, Aberdeenshire]

SCOTTISH HIGHLANDERS, 1725-1775; GRAMPIAN HIGHLANDS, II

FARQUHARSON, JAMES, of Invercauld, Aberdeenshire, letters, 1761-1763, [NRS.E773.49]; 1793-1795. [NRAS.61.6.2]

FARQUHARSON, JOHN, of Kirkton of Aboyne, Aberdeenshire, was served heir to his fatherThomas Farquharson of Kirkton of Aboyne, who died in September 1690, on 2 June 1710. [NRS.S/H]; a Jacobite in 1715, fought at the Siege of Preston. [JAB.61]CRA.47][CS.V.162]

FARQUHARSON, JOHN, of Invercauld, factor for the late Earl of Mar, re lands in Kindrochit and Crathie, Aberdeenshire, 1716. [NRS.E646.2.2]

FARQUHARSON, JOHN, in Attoun, Clova, Angus, sasine, 1716. [NRS.RS35.12/566]

FARQUHARSON, JOHN, of Balmoral, Aberdeenshire, a letter, 1720. [NRS.GD124.15.1206]

FARQUHARSON, JOHN, of Invercauld, Aberdeenshire, writs of the sale of the Davoch of Castleton of Braemar, 1731. [NRS.G124.1.395]

FARQUHARSON, JOHN, farmer in Over Scythy, Lintrathen, a Jacobite in 1745. [OR.4]

FARQUHARSON, JOHN, of Invercauld, Aberdeenshire, letters, 1768. [NRAS.61.6.10]

FARQUHARSON, JOHN, of Kirkton of Aboyne, Aberdeenshire, was served heir to his fatherThomas Farquharson of Kirkton of Aboyne, who died in September 1690, on 2 June 1710. [NRS.S/H]

FARQUHARSON, JOHN, of Invercauld, factor for the late Earl of Mar, re lands in Kindrochit and Crathie, Aberdeenshire, 1716. [NRS.E646.2.2]

FARQUHARSON, JOHN, of Invercauld, lands of Kindrocht in the Lordship of Mar, Aberdeenshire, 1716. [NRS.E646.2.1]

FARQUHARSON, JOHN, of Allanaquoich, lands of Kindrocht in the Lordship of Mar, Aberdeenshire, 1716. [NRS.E646.2.1]

FARQUHARSON, JOHN, of Invercauld, lands of Kindrocht in the Lordship of Mar, Aberdeenshire, 1716. [NRS.E646.2.1]

FARQUHARSON, JOSEPH, of Allanquoich, and his spouse Anna Forbes, a deed, 11 August 1750. [NRS.RF4.176/2.173]

FARQUHARSON, LEWIS, of Achnabride, Lordship of Mar, Aberdeenshire, 1716. [NRS.E646.2.2]

FARQUHARSON, LODOWICK, of Auchindrain, lands of Kindrocht in the Lordship of Mar, Aberdeenshire, 1716. [NRS.E646.2.1]

FARQUHARSON, PATRICK, of Inverey, lands of Kindrocht in the Lordship of Mar, Aberdeenshire, 1716. [NRS.E646.2.1]

FARQUHARSON, PETER, of Tillochcoy, born 1733, died 1801, spouse Isabella Forbes, born 1733, died 1780, parents of George, Francis, and Donald. [Crathie gravestone, Aberdeenshire]

FARQUHARSON, ROBERT, in the parish of Kindrochit, Lordship of Mar, Aberdeenshire, 1716. [NRS.E646.2.1/2]

FARQUHARSON, ROBERT, tenant in Tomnarraw, Lordship of Mar, Aberdeenshire, 1716. [NRS.E646.2.1]

FARQUHARSON, ROBERT, of Finzean, Aberdeenshire, and his eldest son Francis Farquharson, a deed, 1733. [NRS.GD1.584.15]

FARQUHARSON, ROBERT, in Kinaldie, letters, 1757-1759. [NRS.E773.46]

FARQUHARSON, WILLIAM, of Broughdearg, Glen Isla, a Jacobite in 1745. [OR.2]

FARQUHARSON, WILLIAM, a workman in Wester Coull, Lintrathen, a Jacobite in 1745. [OR.25]

FARQUHARSON, WILLIAM, of Bruxie, letters, 1775-1781. [NRS.E773.53]; a bond, 1779. [NRS.E773.63]

FARQUHARSON, WILLIAM, a taxpayer in Balmoral, Crathie, 1799. [ACA]

FARQUHARSON, WILLIAM, of Monaltrie, Aberdeenshire, plans, 1790. [NRS.RHP.3498]

FARQUHARSON, Dr, a taxpayer in Cluny, Crathie, 1799. [ACA]

FARQUHARSON, Captain, a taxpayer in Allanmore, Crathie, 1799. [ACA]

FARQUHARSON, Mr, a taxpayer in Ballater, Glen Muick, 1799. [ACA]

FENTON, DAVID, farmer in Little Kenny, Kingoldrum, a Jacobite in 1745. [OR.4]

FENTON, JAMES, born 1687, in Purgavie, died 1742, husband of Chirsten Johnston, born 1694, died 1746. [Lintrathen gravestone, Angus]

FENTON, JAMES, a workman in Kinclune, Kingoldrum, a Jacobite in 1745. [OR.25]

FENTON, JAMES, in Auchnacree, Fern, Angus, 1770. [NRS.E106.16.5]

FENTON, JOHN, farmer in Purgavie, Lintrathen, a Jacobite in 1745, died in 1789. [OR.25]

FENTON, PETER, of Colhak, Kinnordy, Angus, 1755. [NRS.GD205.29.239]

FENTON, SYLVESTER, a labourer in Liross, Airlie, a Jacobite in 1745. [OR.25]

FENTON, THOMAS, born 1748, a farmer in Ballantore, died 1781, father of John, Peter, and William, [Kingoldrum gravestone, Angus]

FENTON, WILLIAM, of Kirkden, Airlie, Angus, husband of Elspet Low, testament, 1708, Comm. St Andrews. [NRS]

FENTON, WILLIAM, father of Janet Fenton, born 1744, died 1764. [Airlie gravestone, Angus]

FERGUSON, ADAM, minister of Braemar, Aberdeenshire, letters, 1708, 1710. [NRS.GD95.10.23; GD124.15.980]

FERGUSON, CHARLES, born in August 1708, son of Reverend Adam Ferguson and his wife Mary Gordon in Crathie, died in Port Royal, Jamaica, in October 1743. [F.4.189]

FERGUSON, JOHN, tenant, Eastertoun of Dunlappie, Angus, testament, 1784, Comm. Brechin. [NRS]

FERGUSON, JOHN, in Binzion, his relict Elspeth Ferguson in Dillesnaught, Glen Isla, Angus, testament., 1729, Comm. Brechin. [NRS]

FERGUSON, JOSEPH, labourer in Braidston, Airlie, a Jacobite in 1745. [OR.25]

FERRIES, WILLIAM, born 1780, died 1827, husband of Elspet Masson, born 1787, died 1844. [Birse gravestone, Aberdeenshire]

FIFE, Lord, a taxpayer in Mar Lodge, Crathie, 1799. [ACA]

FILP, THOMAS, the younger, a labourer in Lindertis, Airlie, a Jacobite in 1745. [OR.26]

FINDLATOR, JAMES, in Cushnie, appointed Alexander Findlator on Clintesty, as tutor of his son James Findlator on 2 August 1793. [NRS.C22.90.411]

FINDLAY, FRANCIS, in Cortachy, a Jacobite in 1745. [OR.26]

FINDLAY, JOHN, in Edzell, Angus, a deed, 1715. [NRS.RD4.116.59]

FINDLAY, JAMES, born 1765, farmer in Wester Clune, died 1841, husband of Janet Smith, born 1778, died 1829. [Birse gravestone, Aberdeenshire]

FINLAYSON, THOMAS, in the Mill of Innerquharity, Kinnordy, Angus, 1758. [NRS.GD205.29.239]

FITCHET, JOHN, tenant in Blackymill, husband of Margaret Valentine, born 1716, died 1775, parents of Martha, Margaret, Cecilie, John, James, and Cecilie. [Edzell gravestone, Angus]

FLEMING, EDWARD, in Clachglass, Tullich, Lordship of Mar, Aberdeenshire, 1716. [NRS.E646.2.1]

FLEMING, JAMES, minister in Glen Isla, Angus, testament, 1724, Comm. Brechin. [NRS]

FLEMING, JOHN, in Meikle Downie, his relict Isobel Grewar, testament, 1752, Comm. Brechin. [NRS]

FLEMING, PATRICK, in Auchintoull, Glencairn, parish of Tullich, Lordship of Mar, Aberdeenshire, 1716. [NRS.E646.2.1]

FLEMING, PATRICK, in Borland of Blacklunan, Angus, a sasine, 1781. [NRS.RS35.68]

FLETCHER, CHARLES, born 1720, schoolmaster in Migvy, died 23 January 1769, father of Charles, born 1751, schoolmaster in Tarland, died 29 November 1775, William, schoolmaster in Migvy, Lewis and Janet, born 1746, died 25 November 1750. [Migvie gravestone, Aberdeenshire]

FORBES, ALEXANDER, servant to James Craik in Bridgend, Lintrathen, a Jacobite in 1745. [OR.26]

FORBES, ALEXANDER, of Invernan, Aberdeenshire, a memorial, 1775. [NRS.GD124.9.126]

FORBES, ALEXANDER, Captain of the Strathdon Volunteers, papers, 1798-1800. [NRS.GD44.47.46.1]

FORBES, ARTHUR, eldest son of Roderick Forbes of Brux, was served heir to the barony of Towie in the parish of Kinballoch, the davoch of Brux in the parish of Kildrummy, and the lands of Corbanchory in the parish of Cushnie, Aberdeenshire, 1716. [NRS.GD52.599]

FORBES, Sir ARTHUR, of Craigievar, Aberdeenshire, was granted the lands of O'Neill on 19 May 1727, [NRS.RGS.91.118]; testament, 1776, Comm. Aberdeen. [NRS]

FORBES, Sir ARTHUR, of Craigievar, was served heir to Sir Andrew Mitchell of Thainstoun, KCB, British Ambassador in Berlin, on 19 June 1772. [NRS.S/H]

FORBES, CHARLES, in Ballater, a deed, 4 October 1752. [NRS.RD4.178/2.308]

FORBES, DONALD, drummer or piper of the 1st Strathspey Fencible Regiment, 1793. [NRS.GD248.463.1]

FORBES, JOHN, son of Sir John Forbes of Monymusk, Aberdeenshire, was granted the lands of Boyndleyes on 12 February 1712. [NRS.RGS.85.101]

FORBES, JOHN, in Glen Markie, a deed, 1715. [NRS.RD4.116.846]

FORBES, JOHN, drummer or piper of the 1st Strathspey Fencible Regiment, 1793. [NRS.GD248.463.1]

FORBES, JOHN, a taxpayer in Bellimore, Glenbucket, 1799. [ACA]

FORBES, JOHN, a taxpayer in Farmbrake, Glenbucket, 1799. [ACA]

FORBES, WILLIAM, a chapman in Tarland, Aberdeenshire, a deed, 1715. [NRS.RD4.116.241]

FORBES, Sir WILLIAM, of Craigievar, was served heir to his father Sir John Forbes of Craigievar, Aberdeenshire, on 4 August 1716. [NRS.S/H]; a deed, 1715, [NRS.RD2.105.30]; testament, 1723/1727, Comm. Aberdeen. [NRS]

FORBES, WILLIAM, in Bellachallich of Crathie, Aberdeenshire, testament, 1751, Comm. Aberdeen. [NRS]

FORBES, Sir WILLIAM, of Craigievar, was served heir to his father Sir Arthur Forbes of Craigievar who died on 1 January 1773, on 18 August 1773. [NRS.S/H]

FORBES, ...of Tillysnaught, Aberdeenshire, a letter re Tormondlochy, 1754. [NRS.GD1.581.18]

FORRESTER, SYLVESTER, born 1713, son of John Forrester, a workman in Ley, Lintrathen, a Jacobite in 1745. [OR.27]

FORRESTER, WILLIAM, born 1720, son of John Forrester, workman in Kinclune, Kingoldrum, a Jacobite in 1745. [OR.27]

SCOTTISH HIGHLANDERS, 1725-1775; GRAMPIAN HIGHLANDS, II

FORRESTER, WILLIAM, at the East Mill of Glen Isla, Angus, testament, 1774, Comm. Brechin. [NRS]

FORSYTH, HENRY GEORGE, second son of William Forsyth of Harthill minister at Aboyne, Aberdeenshire, a deed, 1793. [NRS.GD52.820]

FORSYTH, JAMES, in Kirkton of Airlie, tack, 1731. [NRS.GD16.Sec.28.225]

FORSYTH, JAMES, a brewer in the Kirkton of Airlie, Angus, 1774. [NRS.GD16.Sec.28.374]

FORSYTH, JOHN, Sergeant of the 1st Strathspey Fencible Regiment, 1793. [NRS.GD248.463.1]

FORSYTH, WILLIAM, minister at Aboyne, Aberdeenshire, a letter, 1711. [NRS.GD52.15.1035]

FORSYTH, WILLIAM, born 1707, son of Alexander Forsyth of Pittodrie, educated at Marischal College, Aberdeen, minister of Aboyne and Glentanar from 1754 until his death in 1793, married Margaret, daughter of John Turner of Turnerhall, parents of William, Margaret, Henry, and John. [F.6.78]

FRASER, DONALD, born 1711, died 1785, spouse Ann Eggo, died 1780. [Crathie gravestone, Aberdeenshire]

FRASER, FRANCIS, of Pitmurchie, born 1649, died 29 April 1718. [Kincardine O'Neil gravestone]

FRASER, FRANCIS, of Findrack, born 22 August 1762, Commander in the Royal Navy and a Post Captain of the Portuguese Navy, died 24 April 1824. [Kincardine O'Neil gravestone, Aberdeenshire]

FRASER, JAMES, Sergeant of the 1st Strathspey Fencible Regiment, 1793. [NRS.GD248.463.1]

FRASER, JAMES, drummer or piper of the 1st Strathspey Fencible Regiment, 1793. [NRS.GD248.463.1]

FRASER, JOHN, born 1733 in Strathdon, Aberdeenshire, enlisted in the Aberdeenshire Fencibles in 1778. [NRS.GD44.47.11]

FRASER, JOHN, session clerk of the parish of Cortachy and Clova, Angus, in 1780. [NRS.CH2.561.3.3]

FRASER, Sir PETER, of Durris, Kincardineshire, rentals, 1730. [NRS.CS181.2254]

FULLERTON, ALEXANDER, a farmer in Edzell, a Jacobite in 1745. [P.2.218]

GAIRDEN, PETER, was granted the lands of Cushnie in 1766. [NRS.SIG1.72.31]

GALL, ALEXANDER, a tenant in Arsellach, Lochlee, Angus, 1716. [NRS.E650.4]

GALL, ALEXANDER, in Auchnacree, was served heir to his uncle James Fenton of Auchnacree, parish of Fearn, Angus, on 22 January 1782. [NRS.S/H]

GALL, JOHN, born 1748, late in Dallyfour, died 26 May 1805, husband of Elisabeth Farquharson, born 1758, died 18 December 1813. [Glen Muick gravestone]

GALL, JOHN, a shoemaker in Dykehead, Cortachy, Angus, testament, 1725, Comm. Brechin. [NRS]

GALLOW, WILLIAM, born 1738, famer in Bogfog, Maryculter, died 21 August 1793, husband of Margaret Walker, born 1743, died 19 April 1831. [Banchory Devenick gravestone, Aberdeenshire]

GALT, ROBERT, in Navar, Angus, 1726. [NRS.CH2.628.17]

GARDEN, CHARLES, of Bellastreen, born before 1671, died 1761; testament subscribed in 1743. [Lochlee gravestone] [NRS.CH2.628.17]

GAULD, WILLIAM, a taxpayer in Netherton, Glenbucket, 1799. [ACA]

GAVIN, WILLIAM, born 1771, miller at Lairney, died 13 August 1849, husband of Elisabeth Smith, born 1772, died at East Lairney on 16 June 1863. [Kincardine O'Neil gravestone]

GERRY, JEAN, in Lethnot, Angus, 1769. [NRS.CH2.628.1.259]

GIBB, ALEXANDER, a tenant in Corrie, Lethnot, Angus, 1716. [NRS.E650.4]

GIBB, DAVID, a tenant in Nether Drumcairn, Lethnot, Angus, 1716, 1722. [NRS.E650.4; CH2.628.17]

GIBB, JOHN, born 1697, tenant farmer in Argeeth, died in 1747, husband of Janet Low, born 1682, died 1746. [Lethnot gravestone]

GIBB, ROBERT, a tenant in Glassrosie, Lethnot, Angus, 1716. [NRS.E650.4]

GIBSON, ..., in Dykehead of Craig, Glen Isla, dead by 1770. [NRS.E106.16.5]

GILBERT, ALEXANDER, drummer or piper of the 1st Strathspey Fencible Regiment, 1793. [NRS.GD248.463.1]

GILBERT, JAMES, Corporal of the 1st Strathspey Fencible Regiment, 1793. [NRS.GD248.463.1]

GILLANDERS, GEORGE, a factor at Aboyne, Aberdeenshire, for the Earl of Aboyne, a letter, 1754. [NRS.GD1.584.17]

GILLESPIE, ALEXANDER, born 1760, farmer in Denhead of Newhills, died 23 January 1843, husband of Elizabeth Harvey, born 1773, died 3 February 1846. [Banchory Ternan gravestone]

GILLIES, JAMES, son of Robert Gillies a merchant in Brechin, minister of Menmuir, Angus, from 1779 to his death in 1783, husband of Ann Durward, parents of Robert, Peter, and Colin. [F.5.408]

GILLIES, JOHN, born 1681, minister of Careston, died in 1753, husband of Mary Watson. [Careston gravestone]

GLASS, DONALD, born 1726, in the Forest of Birse, died 5 March 1797, husband of Helen Ogilvie, born 1742, died 12 March 1801, parents of James Glass, born 1779, died 7 January 1804. [Birse gravestone, Aberdeenshire]

GLASFORD, JOHN, minister at Strathcathro, Angus, testament, 1746, Comm. Brechin. [NRS]

GLENDAY, JAMES, born 1720, son of James Glenday, grieve at Reedie, Airlie, a Jacobite in 1745. [OR.27]

GOLD, ALEXANDER, tenant in Ardgeith, Lethnot and Navar, Angus, testament, 1793, Comm. Brechin. [NRS]

GOLD, ANDREW, a tenant in Reidholes, Lethnot, Angus, 1716. [NRS.E650.4]

GOLD, DAVID, in Auchin, parish of Lochlee, Angus, heir to his uncle Robert Gold in Lichny, 14 October 1757. [NRS.S/H]

GOLD, THOMAS, ruling elder in Lethnot, Angus, 1751. [NRS.CH2.628.1.57]

GORDON, ADAM, of Inverdowie, Aberdeenshire, letters, 1712. [NRS.GD124.15.1066]

GORDON, ADAM, of Comrie, factor on the Aboyne estate, Aberdeenshire, 1714-1729. [NRS.GD181.233]

GORDON, ALEXANDER, of Blelack, Aberdeenshire, a letter, 1705. [NRS.GD124.15.234]

GORDON, ALEXANDER, of Camdall, in part of Stewart's lands of Lossie, Crathie, Lordship of Mar, Aberdeenshire, 1716. [NRS.E646.2.1]

GORDON, ALEXANDER, born 1727, in Little Mill, died 10 March 1809, husband of Jean Smith, born 1741, died 15 November 1800. [Glen Muick gravestone]

GORDON, CHARLES, born 1718 in Banff, graduated MA from Marischal College in 1755, minister of Cortachy and Clova from 1774 to his death in 1795, husband of Rachel Henderson, test., 1795, Comm. Brechin. [NRS][F.5.281]

GORDON, CHARLES, of Abergeldie, Glencairn, Lordship of Mar, Aberdeenshire, 1716. [NRS.E646.2.1/2]

GORDON, CHARLES, of Blelack, Aberdeenshire, a memorial, 1736. [NRS.GD124.8.70]

GORDON, CHARLES, of Braid, factor to the Duke of Gordon, 1790. [NRS.E752.5]

GORDON, CHARLES, of Abergeldie, died in March 1796, husband of Alison Hunter who died in March 1800. [Glen Muick gravestone]

GORDON, CHARLES, a taxpayer in Dorsincilly, Glen Muick, 1799. [ACA]

GORDON, DAVID, tenant of Tillyquhillie, Navar, Angus, rent book, 1757-1772. [NRS.CH2.628.17]

GORDON, HARRY, a servant of the Earl of Aboyne, a contract to build a dyke, 1756. [NRS.GD181.201.2]

GORDON, JAMES, tenant in Milnton of Glen Esk, Angus, 1716. [NRS.E650.4]

GORDON, JAMES, of Banchory, Aberdeenshire, a petition, 1725. [NRS.CS181.2571]

GORDON, JAMES, born 1740, died 9 March 1823. [Kincardine O'Neil gravestone, Aberdeenshire]

GORDON, JAMES, in Lethnot, Angus, 1757. [NRS.CH2.628.1.172]

GORDON, JAMES, died 1754, father of Alexander Gordon, and of Samuel Gordon, born 1750, died 3 December 1798. [Glen Muick gravestone]

GORDON, JOHN, in Tillyquhillie, Navar, Angus, rent book, 1726-1732. [NRS.CH2.628.17]

GORDON, JOHN, factor on the Mar estate, Aberdeenshire, 1716. [NRS.E645.56]

GORDON, JOHN, born 1742 in Cabrach, Aberdeenshire, a farmer, enlisted in the Aberdeenshire Fencibles in 1778. [NRS.GD44.47.11]

GORDON, Captain JOHN, of Glentannar, Aberdeenshire, brother-german of Charles, Earl of Aboyne, and Clementina Lockhart, eldest daughter of George Lockhart of Carnwath, a postnuptial marriage contract, 1761. [NRS.GD1.403.63]

GORDON, NATHANIEL, a taxpayer in Bridgend, Glen Muick, 1799. [ACA]

GORDON, PATRICK, son of Captain Charles Gordon, was granted the lands of Abergeldie, Aberdeenshire, on 7 June 1701. [NRS.RGS.78.75]

GORDON, PETER, born 1764, farmer in Aucholzie, later in Bellamore, died in August 1824, husband of Euphemia Small, born 1759, died in March 1847. [Glen Muick gravestone]

GORDON, PETER, of Abergeldie, born 1751, died 6 December 1819, son of Charles Gordon of Abergeldie. [Glen Muick gravestone, Aberdeenshire]

GORDON, PETER, a taxpayer in Mosstown, Glen Muick, Aberdeenshire, 1799. [ACA]

GORDON, ROBERT, in Raemoir, born 1743, died July 1777, husband of Mary Hogg, born 1745, died 2 February 1833. [Banchory Ternan gravestone, Kincardineshire]

GORDON, ROBERT, in Greenmire, Kinnordy, Angus, 1755. [NRS.GD205.29.239]

GORDON, ROBERT, in Castletoun of Glenlivat, Banffshire, an inhibition, 1793. [NRS.D1.128.1.vii.282]

GORDON, SAMUEL, born 1745, late in Tombreack, died 20 March 1808. [Glenmuick gravestone]

GORDON, THOMAS, portioner of Crochinard, lands of Crathie in the Lordship of Mar, Aberdeenshire, 1716. [NRS.E646.2.1/2]

GORDON, THOMAS, of Crathienaird, born 1743, son of John Gordon and his wife Isobel Shepherd, graduated MA from Marischal College, Aberdeen, 1761, minister of Aboyne and Glentanar from 1784 to 1826, married Elizabeth Michie in 1781, parents of John, Janet, Barbara, George and William. [F.6.78]; letters, 1781-1785. [NRS.E773.44]

GORDON, THOMAS, son of James Gordon of Banchory and Mary Buchan, was baptised in St Paul's, Aberdeen, on

9 December 1746. Witnesses were William Brebner, a merchant, and Alexander Brebner, a surgeon.

GORDON, WILLIAM, son of Alexander Gordon in Knock of Glen Muick, was apprenticed to William Leys a cooper in Aberdeen, for 4 years, 6 July 1792. [ACA]

GORDON, Captain, a taxpayer in Abergeldie, Crathie, 1799. [ACA]

GORDON, Mrs, a taxpayer in Birkhill, Glen Muick, 1799. [ACA]

GOW, DONALD, a workman in Pitewan, Lintrathen, a Jacobite in 1745. [OR.29]

GOWRIE, JOHN, born 1658, miller at Bridgend, Angus, died 1716, husband of Euphan McNab, parents of George, Thomas, Mary, Elizabeth, Katherine, and Jean. [Lintrathen gravestone, Angus]

GRAHAM, or WRIGHT, AGNES, born 1741, died 1818, mother of Robert Wright. [Airlie gravestone]

GRANT, ALAN, in Garvald, a petition, 1768. [NRS]

GRANT, ALAN, Sergeant of the 1st Strathspey Fencible Regiment, 1793. [NRS.GD248.463.1]

GRANT, or BAIN, ALEXANDER, in Connage of Strathspey, testament refers to his wife Elspeth Grant, and his son -in-law John Grant, 1722. [NRS.GD23.4.99]

GRANT, ALPIN, Corporal of the 1st Strathspey Fencible Regiment, 1793. [NRS.GD248.463.1]

GRANT, CHRISTOPHER, eldest son of William Grant of Glenbeg, and Ann Gordon, a deed, 1760. [NRS.GD52.264]

GRANT, DONALD, tenant in Castletoun, Lordship of Mar, Aberdeenshire, 1716. [NRS.E646.2.1]

GRANT, DONALD, Corporal of the 1st Strathspey Fencible Regiment, 1793. [NRS.GD248.463.1]

GRANT, DONALD, drummer or piper of the 1st Strathspey Fencible Regiment, 1793. [NRS.GD248.463.1]

GRANT, DUNCAN, born 1699, late tenant in the Forest of Birse, died 1787, husband of [2?] Elspet McGrigor, born 1741, died 1821, parents of John, Donald born 1724 died 1783, and Alexander, born 1761, died 1808. [Birse gravestone, Aberdeenshire]

GRANT, DUNCAN, born 1709, tenant in the Forest of Birse, died 1787, husband of Elspet McGregor, born 1741, died 1821, parents of John, Donald born 1724, died 1783, and Alexander, born 1761, died 1808. [Birse gravestone]

GRANT, GRIZEL, daughter of James Grant of Rothiemurchus, and spous e of Alexander Cumming of Logie, a sasine, 1750. [NRS.RS29.VI.497]

GRANT, JAMES, of Tullochgriban, factor on the Strathspey estate, 1762-1763. [NRS.GD248.42.3]

GRANT, JAMES, in Garvald, a petition, 1768. [NRS]

GRANT, JAMES, clerk at Castle Grant, in 1770s. [NRS.GD248.45.4]

GRANT, JAMES, Corporal of the 1st Strathspey Fencible Regiment, 1793. [NRS.GD248.463.1]

GRANT, JOHN, tenant in Bellachlon, Lordship of Mar, Aberdeenshire, 1716. [NRS.E646.2.1]

GRANT, JOHN, husband of Margaret Christie, born 1675, died 1754, parents of David Grant, farmer at Fichill, died 1773. [Cortachy gravestone, Angus]

GRANT, JOHN, born 1736, died 9 May 1799. [Kincardine O'Neil gravestone, Aberdeenshire]

GRANT, JOHN, of Bellimore, chamberlain of Strathspey, 1750s. [NRS.GD248.14.1]; will, 1789. [NRS.GD248.246.10]

GRANT, JOHN, husband of Margaret Christie, born 1675, died 1754, parents of David Grant, farmer at Fichill, died 1773. [Cortachy gravestone, Angus]

GRANT, JOHN, Corporal of the 1st Strathspey Fencible Regiment, 1793. [NRS.GD248.463.1]

GRANT, JOHN, [1], Sergeant of the 1st Strathspey Fencible Regiment, 1793. [NRS.GD248.463.1]

GRANT, JOHN, [2], Sergeant of the 1st Strathspey Fencible Regiment, 1793. [NRS.GD248.463.1]

GRANT, JOHN, of Kincardine O'Neil, born 136, died 9 May 1799. [Kincardine O'Neil gravestone]

GRASSICK, JAMES, born 1745 in Strathdon, Aberdeenshire, , enlisted in the Aberdeenshire Fencibles in 1778. [NRS.GD44.47.11]

GRAY, WILLIAM, born 1757 in Fetteresso, Kincardineshire, a brazier, enlisted in the Aberdeenshire Fencibles in 1778. [NRS.GD44.47.11]

GRAY, Mrs, a taxpayer in Balgairn, Glen Muick, Aberdeenshire, 1799. [ACA]

GREIRSON, JOHN, a merchant in Charleston of Aboyne, Aberdeenshire, a bond, 1749. [NRS.CS229.MG7.60]

GREWER, DONALD, portioner of Achalader, lands of Crathie in the Lordship of Mar, Aberdeenshire, 1716. [NRS.E646.2.1]

GREWAR, JOHN, in Dalvaine, Glen Isla, Angus, testament, 1729, Comm. Brechin. [NRS]

GREWAR, PETER, born 1733, tenant in the Forest of Birse, died 1811, husband of Janet Sandysen, born 1748, died 1822. [Birse gravestone, Aberdeenshire]

GRANT, LEWIS, chamberlain of Strathspey, 1721-1722. [NRS.GD248.109.1]

GRANT, PATRICK, was granted the lands of Rothiemurcus on 22 June 1713. [NRS.RGS.86.53]

GRANT, PATRICK, tenant in Tomnarraw, Lordship of Mar, Aberdeenshire, 1716. [NRS.E646.2.1]

GRANT, PETER, Sergeant of the 1st Strathspey Fencible Regiment, 1793. [NRS.GD248.463.1]

GRANT, PETER, drummer or piper of the 1st Strathspey Fencible Regiment, 1793. [NRS.GD248.463.1]

GRANT, ROBERT, in Auchterblair, a letter, 1771. [NRS.GD248.45.4]

GRANT, ROBERT, Corporal of the 1st Strathspey Fencible Regiment, 1793. [NRS.GD248.463.1]

GRANT, THOMAS, born 1729, farmer in Ley, died 1780, husband of Agnes Strachan, born 1726, died 1801. [Banchory Ternan gravestone]

GRANT, WILLIAM, born 1701, farmer in Gateside, died 2 August 1781, husband of Janet Smith, born 1707, died 4 April 1787, son James Grant born 1740, died 14 May 1783. [Strachan gravestone, Kincardineshire]

GRANT, Colonel WILLIAM, was granted the lands of Ballindalloch on 13 February 1727. [NRS.RGS.92.16]

GRANT, WILLIAM, was served heir to his father Captain Alexander Grant of Ballindalloch on 18 July 1751. [NRS.S/H]

GRANT, WILLIAM, of Delchapple, baron bailie of Strathspey, petitions, 1784-1786. [NRS.GD248.432.7]

GRANT, WILLIAM, drummer or piper of the 1st Strathspey Fencible Regiment, 1793. [NRS.GD248.463.1]

GREGORIE, MALCOLM, 'one of Aboyne's men', a Jacobite in 1715. [NRS.GD45.1.201]

GREIG, ALEXANDER, born 1722, farmer in Hatton, ded 18 November 1794, husband of Margaret, born 1725, died 10 November 1794, parents of Isabella, born 1758, died 9 April 1788. [Banchory Ternan gravestone]

GREWER, DONALD, portioner of Achalader, lands of Crathie in the Lordship of Mar, Aberdeenshire, 1716. [NRS.E646.2.1]

SCOTTISH HIGHLANDERS, 1725-1775; GRAMPIAN HIGHLANDS, II

GREWER, GEORGE, a labourer in Glen Isla, a Jacobite in 1745, transported to the colonies in 1747. [P.2.268]

GREWAR, JOHN, in Dalvaine, Glen Isla, testament, 1729, Comm. Brechin. [NRS]

GRIERSON, ALEXANDER, of Innereing, parish of Glencairn, Aberdeenshire, 1716. [NRS.E646.2.2]

GREIRSON, JOHN, a merchant in Charleston of Aboyne, Aberdeenshire, a bond, 1749. [NRS.CS229.MG7.60]

GRUAR, ALASTAR, in the parish of Kindrochit, Lordship of Mar, Aberdeenshire, 1716. [NRS.E646.2.2]

GRUARS, JAMES, in Netherton of Craig, Glen Isla, 1770. [NRS.E106.16.5]

GRUARS, JOHN, in Netherton of Craig, Glen Isla, Angus, 1770. [NRS.E106.16.5]

GUTHRIE, DAVID, in Balconnel, Menmuir, Angus, 1770. [NRS.E106.16.5]

HAMILTON, ANDREW, son of Alexander Hamilton of Kinkell, graduated MA from St Andrews in 1693, minister of Navar, Angus, from 1713 to his death in 1714, testament, 1714, Comm. Brechin. [NRS][F.5.401]

HAMILTON, HENRY, MA, minister of Navar, Angus, from 1708 to 1712. [F.5.401]

HANTON, JOHN, in the Inch, Kinnordy, Angus, 1756. [NRS.GD205.29.239]

HANTON, ROBERT, died in the Stron 1794, husband of Jean Lindsay, died 1807. [Glen Prosen gravestone, Angus]

HARPER, ROBERT, born 1711, farmer in Miltown of Tillysnaght, died 1795, husband of Christian Ewen, born 1715, died 1788, parents of Hugh Harper, born 1747, farmer in Milltown of Tillynaught, died 1830. [Birse gravestone, Aberdeenshire]

HARPER, ROBERT, born 1734, tenant in Arntilly, died 1798, husband of Jane Middleton, born 1739, died 1834, parents of Robert Harper, born 1770, died 1801. [Birse gravestone, Aberdeenshire]

HAY, ALEXANDER, Sergeant of the 1st Strathspey Fencible Regiment, 1793. [NRS.GD248.463.1]

HAY, WILLIAM, born 1731, tenant in Inverscandly, died 1813, husband of Mary Mitchell, born 1743, died 1825, parents of John, Alexander, Charles, Janet, Ann, Isabella, Mary, George, James, and David. [Edzell gravestone, Angus]

HAY, WILLIAM, at the Manse of Midmar, cautioner of John Hay an apprentice baker in 1801. [ACA]

HENDERSON, JAMES, in Westerton of Easter Derry, Glen Isla, Angus, 1770. [NRS.E106.16.5]

HENDERSON, WILLIAM, gardener in Edzell, Angus, and tenant of Slateford, 1760s. [Edzell gravestone]

HENDRY, CHARLES, born 1740, died at Gella in 1827. [Cortachy gravestone, Angus]

HENDRY, THOMAS, in Lethnot, Angus, 1749. [NRS.CH2.628.1]

HENDRY, THOMAS, tenant in Blackhaugh, Navar and Lethnot, Angus, 1769. [NRS.GD45.18.1997]

HENDRY, WILLIAM, a labourer in Glenbucket, Aberdeenshire, was impressed into military service in 1757. [ACA.as.amil.2.17]

HENRY, JOHN, of Gaillay, Cortachy, Angus, testament, 1713, Comm. Brechin. [NRS]

HILL, JOHN, in Cotton of Craig, Glen Isla, 1770. [NRS.E106.16.5]

HOLBERT, WILLIAM, born 1721, servant Pitcarity, died 1786. [Glen Prosen gravestone]

HOOD, WILLIAM, born 1702, in Nether Logie, died 1758, husband of Elspeth Rattray. [Airlie gravestone]

HOWE, ALEXANDER, grieve in Cortachy, Angus, testament, 1792, Comm. Brechin. [NRS]

HOWE, DAVID, tenant in Crossboig and in the Mill of Rottall, Angus, 1773. [NRS.GD16.Sec.16.372]

HOWE, JAMES, in Nether Handick, Glen Ogilvy, Angus, a sasine, 1772. [NRS.RS35.24]

HUNTER, WILLIAM, husband of Jean Watt, in Banchory, Aberdeenshire, an army reservist in 1804. [ACA.AS.AMI.6.1.1]

HURRY, WILLIAM, born 1740, died 1 April 1805, husband of Elisabeth Jaffrey, born 1769, died 6 October 1822. [Kincardine O'Neil gravestone, Aberdeenshire]

HUTCHIN, JAMES, of the Inch, Kinnordy, Angus, 1756. [NRS.GD205.29.239]

HUTCHINSON, JAMES, glover in the Milton of Kingoldrum, a sasine 171705. [NRS.RS35.11.70]

HUTCHISON, JAMES, a smith at the Bridgend of Cortachy, Angus, a sasine, 1776. [NRS.RS35.26]

HUTCHISON, JOHN, Sergeant of the 1st Strathspey Fencible Regiment, 1793. [NRS.GD248.463.1]

INGLIS, Mrs CHRISTIAN, born 1736, died 1808. [Lochlee gravestone, Angus]

INNERDALE, JANET, in Skellie, Lochlee, Angus, 1758, testament, Comm. Brechin. [NRS]

INNERDALE, JOHN, in Kirn, Lochlee, Angus, testament, 1753, Comm. Brechin. [NRS]

INNES, JOHN, of Sinnahard, Aberdeenshire, chamberlain to the Earl of Mar, a letter, 1710. [NRS.GD124.15.9741]

INNES, JOHN, a tenant of the Mill of Lethnot, Angus, testament, 1749, Comm. Brechin. [NRS]

IRVINE, ALEXANDER, a tack of the Mains of Kincragie in the parish of Tarland, Aberdeenshire, 1701. [NRS.GD33.52.19]

SCOTTISH HIGHLANDERS, 1725-1775; GRAMPIAN HIGHLANDS, II

IRVINE, JAMES, factor of Durris, Kincardineshire, a deed, 1730. [NRS.CS165.857]

JACK, ADAM, a servant in Glen Isla, Angus, an inhibition, 1800. [NRS.D1.128.1. xlviii.338]

JACK, DAVID, slater in Fettercairn, Kincardineshire, an inhibition, 1790. [NRS.D1.128.1.v.83]

JACK, WALTER, Sergeant of the 1st Strathspey Fencible Regiment, 1793. [NRS.GD248.463.1]

JAMIESON, MARGARET, in Weard Head, died 1798. [Glen Muick gravestone, Aberdeenshire]

JAMIESON, MARGARET, in Weard Head, died 1805. [Glen Muick gravestone, Aberdeenshire]

JOHNSTON, JAMES, born 1738, late of Hill of Inchmarlo, died 22 February 1807, husband of Jean Innes, born 1739, died 1808, parents of Andrew, born 1787, died 12 September 1816. [Banchory Ternan gravestone]

JOHNSTON, GEORGE, in Balfour, Angus, factor to Lord Panmure, a Jacobite in 1745. [LPR.218][P.2.304]

JOHNSTON, JAMES, in Balbridy, Kinnordy, Angus, 1759. [NRS.GD205.29.239]

JOLLY, DAVID, born 1755, died in Kinminity 1833, husband of Isabel Findlay, born 1765, died 1847. [Birse gravestone, Aberdeenshire]

JOLLIE, JAMES, tenant of the Mill of Auchian, Lochlee, 1716. [NRS.E650/4]

JOLLIE, THOMAS, tenant in Skour, Lochlee, Angus, 1716. [NRS.E650/4]

KEIR, ALEXANDER, in the parish of Glencair, Lordship of Mar, Aberdeenshire, 1716. [NRS.E646.2.2]

KEIR, DUNCAN, portioner of Stranotten, parish of Glencairn, Lordship of Mar, Aberdeenshire, 1716. [NRS.E646.2.2]

KEIR, JAMES, in Rynlein and Stanlea, Glencairn, Lordship of Mar, Aberdeenshire, 1716. [NRS.E646.2.1]

KERR, ALEXANDER, at Cuish of Kildrummy, Aberdeenshire, a letter, 1730. [NRS.GD124.15.1366]

KEITH, JOHN, born 1731, farmer in the Mains of Banchory, died 14 April 1817. [Banchory Devenick gravestone]

KENNY, JAMES, in Little Inch, Kinnordy, Angus, 1755. [NRS.GD205.29.239]

KEITH, MARY, relict of John Ogilvy of Incheuan, a deed, 8 May q750. [NRS.RD3.211/2.176]

KERR, ALEXANDER, at Cuish of Kildrummy, Aberdeenshire, a letter, 1730. [NRS.GD124.15.1366]

KERR, JOHN, a farmer in Loinmore, husband of Elizabeth Coutts who died in May 1727. [Glen Muick gravestone]

KER, ROBERT, born 1707, son of Reverend James Ker in Dun, ordained in Lethnot in 1717, then minister at Lochlee from 1723 to 1728, died in 1735, testament, 1735, Comm. Brechin. [NRS][F.5.399/401]

KILGOUR, PETER, Sergeant of the 1st Strathspey Fencible Regiment, 1793. [NRS.GD248.463.1]

KINDLY, THOMAS, in Lethnot, Angus, in 1758. [NRS.CH2.628.1.177]

KINLOCH, ..., of Kilry, Glen Isla, Angus, 1770. [NRS.E106.16.5]

KINNEAR, ALEXANDER, a tailor in Dilladies, Fettercairn, husband of Mary Jack, sasines. 1773. [NRS.RS35.24.24/494]

KINNEAR, DAVID, tenant in Auchforthe, Lochlee, 1716. [NRS.E650/4]

KINNEAR, PETER, a labourer in Glen Ogilvy, a Jacobite in 1745. [OR.34]

KINNEAR, THOMAS, tenant in Inchgeomidle, Lochlee, 1716. [NRS.E650/4]

KINNEAR, THOMAS, farmer in Milton of Glen Esk, a Jacobite in 1745. [OR.34]

KNOWLES, JOHN, died 1776, husband of Margart Collie, died 1799, parents of Elspet Knowles, born 1758, died 2 July 1826. [Banchory-Devenick gravestone, Aberdeenshire]

KNOLS, WILLIAM, born 1678, tenant in Legart, died 9 December 1748, husband of Jean, born 1677, died 3 December 1745, parents of Isobel, born 1721, and John, born 1699, died 28 March 1751. [Banchory Devenick gravestone]

LACKIE, ALEXANDER, workman in Kingoldrum, a Jacobite in 1745. [OR.34]

LAING, ANDREW, in the Mill of Innerarity, Kinnordy, Angus, 1755. [NRS.GD205.29.239]

LAING, JAMES, in Drumcairn, parish of Lethnot, husband of Anne Gibb, born 1689, died 1737. [Lethnot gravestone]

LAING, MARGARET, in Lethnot, 1759. [NRS.CH2.628.1.110]

LAMONT, DONALD, in the parish of Kindrochit, Lordship of Mar, Aberdeenshire, 1716. [NRS.E646.2.2]

LAMONT, DONALD, born 1767, died at Shanvel in 1824, spouse Hellen Farquharson died 1833. [Braemar gravestone, Aberdeenshire]

LAMONT, JOHN, in the parish of Kindrochit, Lordship of Mar, Aberdeenshire, 1716. [NRS.E646.2.2]

LAMONT, MALCOLM, in the parish of Kindrochit, Lordship of Mar, Aberdeenshire, 1716. [NRS.E646.2.2]

LAMONT, MARGARET, in Castleton in the parish of Kindrochit, Lordship of Mar, Aberdeenshire, 1716. [NRS.E646.2.2]

LAMONT, WILLIAM, in the parish of Kindrochit, Lordship of Mar, Aberdeenshire, 1716. [NRS.E646.2.2]

SCOTTISH HIGHLANDERS, 1725-1775; GRAMPIAN HIGHLANDS, II

LAW, ARTHUR, born 1762, farmer in the Milton of Lairney, died 23 December 1835, his wife Isabel Berrie, born 1768, died 14 January 1840. [Kincardine O'Neil gravestone]

LAWSON, JAMES, born 1725, workman in Wester Coull, Lintrathen, a Jacobite in 1745, transported to the West Indies in 1747. [P.2.234][OR.34][TNA.SP36.102][LPR.220]

LAWSON, JOHN, tenant in Bogtoun, Lethnot, 1716. [NRS.E650/4]

LAWSON, JOHN, tenant in Clockie, Lethnot, 1716. [NRS.E650/4]

LAWSON, JOHN, born 1758 in Alford, Aberdeenshire, a laborer, enlisted in the Aberdeenshire Fencibles in 1778. [NRS.GD44.47.11]

LAWSON, PETER, miller at th Bridgend of Lintrathen, a Jacobite in 1745. [OR.35][LPR.220]

LEIGHTON, ALEXANDER, in Drumcairn, Navar and Lethnot, 1770. [NRS.GD45.18.2016]

LEIGHTON, JAMES, born 1730, tenant in Drumcairn 1769, died 1795, husband of Janet Black, born 1747, died 1783. [Lethnot gravestone] [NRS.CH2.628.1.245]

LEIGHTON, ROBERT, born 1771, tenant in Drumcairn, died 1798. [Lethnot gravestone, Angus]

LEITCH, DAVID, born 1735, son of John Leitch tenant in Bonnington, drowned in the West Water during 1757. [Lethnot gravestone, Angus]

LEITCH, JOHN, born 1737, son of John Leitch tenant in Bonnington, drowned in the West Water during 1757. [Lethnot gravestone, Angus]

LEITH, ALEXANDER, of Glenkindie, Kincardineshire, a bond, 1760. [NRS.GD52.264]

LESLIE, DAVID, born 1768, wright to the Earl of Aboyne, died 26 August 1819, husband of Isabel Bell, parents of Janet, David, and Mary. [Aboyne gravestone]

LESLIE, WILLIAM, born 1758 in Rhynie, Aberdeenshire, a mill wright, enlisted in the Aberdeenshire Fencibles in 1778. [NRS.GD44.47.11]

LEUCHARS, JAMES, in Glen Esk, a Jacobite in 1745. [OR.9]

LEYS, WILLIAM, son of Francis Leys at Inver Aberarder, parish of Mey, was apprenticed to Alexander Morison a cooper in Aberdeen, for 5 years, 15 May 1783. Cautioner was Francis Leys in Inverall. [ACA]

LIDDELL, THOMAS, Corporal of the 1st Strathspey Fencible Regiment, 1793. [NRS.GD248.463.1]

LIGHTON, DAVID, born 1722, tenant in Shanford, died 1794. [Fern gravestone, Angus]

LINDSAY, ALEXANDER, of Over Lethnot, Angus, 1715. [NRS.GD16.13.64]

LINDSAY, ALEXANDER, of Rottall, a sasine, 1726. [NRS.RS35.14.155]

LINDSAY, ALEXANDER, graduated MA from King's College, Aberdeen, 1674, minister at Cortachy from 1687 to 1690 died 1729, husband of Jean Dall, parents of James, Mary, Elizabeth, and Isobel, testament, 1723, Comm. Brechin. [NRS][F.5.280];a deeds, 1707. [NRS.RD4.100.670/688]

LINDSAY, ALEXANDER, son of the late George Lindsay of Lethnot, and a sailor, testament, 1727, Comm. Edinburgh. [NRS]

LINDSAY, ANDREW, tenant in Auchian, Lochlee, Angus, 1716. [NRS.E650/4]

LINDSAY, CHARLES, a taxpayer in Milltown, Glenbucket, Aberdeenshire, 1799. [ACA]

LINDSAY, DAVID, of Edzell, Angus, deeds, 1724. [NRS.GD3.14.2.1.36/38]

LINDSAY, DAVID, of Edzell, relict Jean Fullerton, testament, 1718, Comm. Brechin. [NRS]; deeds, 1724. [NRS.GD3.14.2.1.36/38]

LINDSAY, DAVID, in Fetteragie, testament, 1778, Comm. Brechin. [NRS]

LINDSAY, GEORGE, of Lethnot, a sasine, 1726. [NRS.RS35.14.95]

LINDSAY, ISOBEL, daughter of Alexander Lindsay, minister at Cortachy, formerly a schoolmaster, and relict of William Bowar of Kinnettles, sasine, 1747. [NRS.RS35.17.376/499]

LINDSAY, JAMES, was served heir to his grand-father Robert Lindsay of Glenqueich in the Lordship and Barony of Rescobie, 17 April 1759. [NRS.S/H]

LINDSAY, JEAN, spouse of Thomas Mll in Dykehead of Cortachy, a sasine, 1711. [NRS.R35.12.130]

LINDSAY, JOHN, of Glaplet, Cortachy, Angus, testament, 1712, Comm. Brechin. [NRS]

LINDSAY, JOHN, parson of Lethnot, Angus, 1715. [NRS.RD4.116.575]

LINDSAY, JOHN, of Invermark, Angus, a letter, 1715. [NRS.GD45.216]

LINDSAY, Mr JOHN, tenant in Innerascraty, Lochlee, 1716. [NAS.E650/4]

LINDSAY, JOHN, of Pitscandly, Rescobie, Angus, a Jacobite in 1715. [USA.Cheap ms5.537][NRS.E652]

LINDSAY, JOHN, tenant in Tulliebarns, 1716, in Lethnot, Angus, 1722. [NRS.E650/4; CH2.628.17]

LINDSAY, JOHN, late tenant in Tulliebardin, Lethnot, Angus, his widow Margaret Duncan, testament, 1741, Comm. Brechin. [NRS]

LINDSAY, JOHN, born 1763, tenant in Lethnot, died 1837, husband of Agnes Findlay, born 1766, died 1837. [Cortachy gravestone, Angus]

LINDSAY, ROBERT, in Dykehead of Cortachy, and John Milne a servant of the laird of Clova, a bond, 1707. [NRS.GD16.42.675]

LINDSAY, ROBERT, an Episcopalian preacher in Edzell, deposed in 1716. [NRS.CH2.575.1]; a sasine, 1709. [NRS.RS35.10.463]

LINDSAY, ROBERT, in Romants, Cortachy, testament, 1750, Comm. Brechin. [NRS]

LINDSAY, ROBERT, tenant in the Mill of Rottall, 1757. [NRS.GD16.Sec.28/356]

LINDSAY, THOMAS, born 1754, farmer at Rottal, Angus, died 1835. [Clova gravestone, Angus]

LINDSAY, WALTER, tenant in Lochlee, Angus, 1716. [NRS.E650/4]

LINDSAY, WILLIAM, and his son William, in Over Lethnot, Angus, 1715. [NRS.GD16.13.645.]

LINDSAY, WILLIAM, of Woodend in Glenprosen, sasines, 1761, 1774. [NRS.RS35.19.293; RS35.25.50]

LINDSAY, ..., born 1699, tenant in Nether Agie, Angus, died 1778, husband of Jean Lucas, born 1728, died 1777. [Clova gravestone, Angus]

LINDSAY, ..., in Glenquich, 1736. [NRS.RHP#1170/1-2]

LOGIE, PETER, tailor in Tigerton, Menmuir, a Jacobite in 1745. [P.3.346]

LONDON, DAVID, son of William London and his wife Jean Miller, husband of Margaret Dougall, born 1740, died 1774. [Lintrathen gravestone, Angus]

LONG, JAMES, in Lethnot, Angus, 1722. [NRS.CH2.628.17]

LOTHIAN, JOHN, a ploughman in Easter Peel, Lintrathen, a Jacobite in 1745. [OR.35]

LOUSON, JOHN, in Lethnot, Angus, 1722. [NRS.CH2.628/17]

LOW, DAVID, tenant in Buskland, Lochlee, 1716. [NRS.E650/4]

LOW, DAVID, the elder, tenant in Auchian, Lochlee, 1716. [NRS.E650/4]

LOW, DAVID, the younger, tenant in Auchian, Lochlee, 1716. [NRS.E650/4]

LOW, DAVID, born 1713, tenant in Sandyhillock, died 1748, testament, 1748, Comm. St Andrews; husband of Isobel Nedry. [Edzell gravestone, Angus]

LOW, FRANCIS, tenant in Woodside of Dunlappie, relict Janet Fairweather, testament, 1747, Comm. Brechin. [NRS]

LOW, FRANCIS, born 1765, died 16 June 1826, husband of Margaret Ross, born 1776, died 27 July 1853. [Birse gravestone]

LOW, JAMES, and his son James, tenant farmers in the Newton of Lintrathen, 1720. [NRS.GD16.Sec.28/329]

LOW, JAMES, in Culhaugh, tenant of the Mill of Quiech, 1751. [NRS.GD16.Sec.28/352]

LOW, JAMES, servant at Cortachy, husband of Christian Edward, 1776. [NRS.GD16.Sec.41/966]

LOW, JOHN, tenant in Arsellach, Lochlee, Angus, 1716. [NRS.E650/4]

LOW, THOMAS, a 'tyler' in Gallie Hill, husband of Catherine Lunan, born 1672, died 1749. [Airlie gravestone, Angus]

LOW, THOMAS, tenant in Arsellach, Lochlee, Angus, 1716. [NRS.E650/4]

LOW, WILLIAM, in Lethnott, Angus, 1758. [NRS.CH2.628.1.234]

LOWDON, JAMES, in Ballacks, Glen Isla, Angus, testament.,1714, Comm. Brechin. [NRS]

LUMSDANE, JOHN, of Cushney, Aberdeenshire, an inhibition, 1781. [NRS.D1.128.1.lxxvi.174]

LUMSDANE, ROBERT, in Corrachie, Aberdeenshire, inhibitions, 1785. [NRS.D1.128.1.lxxvi.296/297]

LUMSDEN, DAVID, son of William Lumsden of Titboutie, Aberdeenshire, 1722. [NRS.GD33.52.21]

LUMSDEN, HARRY, of Auchindoir, a Jacobite in 1715, captured at the Siege of Preston, transported to Maryland in 1716, returned to Scotland, died at Kildrummy in 1754. [SPC.1716.311][HM.387][NRS.GD1.53.72]

LUMSDEN, HARRY, son of William Lumsden in Mid Clova, was apprenticed to Adam Baxter a cooper in Aberdeen, for 6 years, 1755. [ACA]

LUMSDEN, JAMES, minister of Strathdon, Aberdeenshire, a letter, 1739. [NRS.GD124.15.1497]

LUMSDEN, JAMES, of Corrachee, Aberdeenshire, a sasine re the mill of Tarland, Aberdeenshire, 1729. [NRS.GD33.52.10]

LUMSDEN, JAMES, of Cushnie, Aberdeenshire, a deed, 1772. [NRS.GD52.765]

LUMSDEN, JOHN, gardener at Castle Forbes, cautioner for Forbes Davidson an apprentice in 1798. [ACA]

LUMSDEN, ROBERT, of Corrachee, Aberdeenshire, a sasine re the mill of Tarland, Aberdeenshire, 1707. [NRS.GD33.52.89]

LUNAN, JAMES, weaver in Purgavie, Lintrathen, a Jacobite in 1745. [OR.36]

LUNDIE, THOMAS, in Gobbintore, Glen Isla, testament,1723, Comm. Brechin. [NRS]

LYALL, JOHN, born 1749, tenant in Burnsaugart, died 1826, husband of Violet Carnegie, born 1760, died 1834. [Edzell gravestone, Angus]

LYON, GRIZEL, relict of James Paton at the Mill of Cortachy, Angus, a deed, 1730. [NRS.GD16.42.712]

LYON, JAMES, son of Frederick Lyon minister at Airlie, Angus, a Jacobite in 1715, fought at Sheriffmuir. [CAT.II.205]

LYON, MARJORY, in Grantown on Spey, Morayshire, in 1768. [NRS.GD248.45.4]

SCOTTISH HIGHLANDERS, 1725-1775; GRAMPIAN HIGHLANDS, II

LYON, WILLIAM, the elder, of Easter Ogill, Angus, husband of Margaret Colville, testament, 1719, Comm. Brechin. [NRS]

LYON, WILLIAM, of Easter Ogill, Angus, testament, 1724, Comm. Brechin. [NRS]

LYON, ..., son of George Lyon minister of Tannadice, Angus, a Jacobite hung in 1716. [F.3.305]

LYON, ..., of Wester Ogil, Angus, 1736. [NRS.RHP#1170/1-2]

MCALPIN, PETER, tenant in Tomintoul, Moray, with two sons in the service of the East India Company, 1776. [NRS.GD44.23.33.2]

MCANDREW, JAMES, died 1788, spouse Isabel Middleton. [Crathie gravestone, Aberdeenshire]

MCARA, DUNCAN, minister at Logerait, a letter, 1756. [NRS.E783.46]

MACARRA, JAMES, a servant in Balnakeely, Lintrathen, a Jacobite in 1745. [OR.37]

MCARDIE, ROBERT, in the parish of Kindrochit, Lordship of Mar, Aberdeenshire, 1716. [NRS.E646.2.2]

MCBAIN, HUGH, Sergeant of the 1st Strathspey Fencible Regiment, 1793. [NRS.GD248.463.1]

MCCONACH, ROBERT, born 1769, farmer in Birsebegg, died 1847, husband of Isabel Watt born 1771, died 1830. [Birse gravestone, Aberdeenshire]

MCDONALD, ALEXANDER, [1], Sergeant of the 1st Strathspey Fencible Regiment, 1793. [NRS.GD248.463.1]

MCDONALD, ALEXANDER, [2], Sergeant of the 1st Strathspey Fencible Regiment, 1793. [NRS.GD248.463.1]

MCDONALD, COLLEN, born 1736, died 1811, father of Donald, James, and William. [Cortachy gravestone, Angus]

MCDONALD, DONALD, Sergeant of the 1st Strathspey Fencible Regiment, 1793. [NRS.GD248.463.1]

MCDONALD, DONALD, in Mill of Cosh, wife Margaret Frquharson born 1749, died 1812, parents of Charles McDonald born 1785, died 1811. [Braemar gravestone, Aberdeenshire]

MCDONALD, DONALD, Corporal of the 1st Strathspey Fencible Regiment, 1793. [NRS.GD248.463.1]

MCDONALD, DUNCAN, Sergeant of the 1st Strathspey Fencible Regiment, 1793. [NRS.GD248.463.1]

MCDONALD, EWAN, Sergeant of the 1st Strathspey Fencible Regiment, 1793. [NRS.GD248.463.1]

MCDONALD, FRANCIS, factor of Invercauld, Aberdeenshire, died 15 March 1773. [NRAS.61.21.1]

MACDONALD, JAMES, factor for the forfeited estate of Glenbucket, accounts, 1758-1764. [NRS.E752.14]

MCDONALD, JOHN, of Rienetton of Glencairn parish, Lordship of Mar, Aberdeenshire, 1716. [NRS.E646.2.2]

MCDONALD, JOHN, born 1739, farmer in Aldvaig, died 1808. [Braemar gravestone, Aberdeenshire]

MCDONALD, JOHN, Sergeant of the 1st Strathspey Fencible Regiment, 1793. [NRS.GD248.463.1]

MCDONALD, ROBERT, Corporal of the 1st Strathspey Fencible Regiment, 1793. [NRS.GD248.463.1]

MCDONALD, WILLIAM, in Rincanton, Remicras, and Lynfork, Tullich, Lordship of Mar, Aberdeenshire, 1716. [NRS.E646.2.1]

MCDONALD, WILLIAM, in Westermicras, Tullich, Lordship of Mar, Aberdeenshire, 1716. [NRS.E646.2.1]

MCDONALD, Captain, a taxpayer in Rineton, Glen Muick, 1799. [ACA]

MCDONELL, ANDREW, Corporal of the 1st Strathspey Fencible Regiment, 1793. [NRS.GD248.463.1]

SCOTTISH HIGHLANDERS, 1725-1775; GRAMPIAN HIGHLANDS, II

MCDONELL, ANGUS, Corporal of the 1st Strathspey Fencible Regiment, 1793. [NRS.GD248.463.1]

MCDONEL, DONALD, and his wife Margaret Duff, 1733. [Lochlee gravestone]

MCDONEL, JOHN, and his wife Margaret Tohou, 1733. [Lochlee gravestone]

MCDOUGAL, COLIN, born 1748, died 1819, husband of Elizabeth McKenzie, born 1744, died 1821. [Glen Isla gravestone]

MCDOUGALL, LACHLAN, in Milnton of Blacklunans, Angus, a sasine, 1741. [NRS.RS35.XVI.79]

MCDUGAL, JOHN, born 1740, died 1812. [Braemar gravestone, Aberdeenshire]

MACGILLIVIE, ALEXANDER, tenant in Milne of Castletoun, Lordship of Mar Aberdeenshire, 1716. [NRS.E646.2.1]

MACGILLIVIE, CALLUM, tenant in Milne of Castletoun, Lordship of Mar, Aberdeenshire, 1716. [NRS.E646.2.1]

MCGILLIVIE, CALLUM, tenant in Ardchie, Lordship of Mar, Aberdeenshire, 1716. [NRS.E646.2.1]

MCGILLIVIE, DONALD, tenant in Castletoun, Lordship of Mar, Aberdeenshire, 1716. [NRS.E646.2.1]

MCGILLIVIE, DONALD, tenant in Ardchie, Lordship of Mar, Aberdeenshire, 1716. [NRS.E646.2.1]

MCGILLIVIE, JOHN, officer of the Lordship of Mar, Aberdeenshire, 1716. [NRS.E646.2.1]

MCGILLIVIE, JOHN, the younger, tenant in Castletoun, Lordship of Mar, Aberdeenshire, 1716. [NRS.E646.2.1]

MCGILLIVIE, JOHN, miller at Castleton of Braemar, Aberdeenshire, a letter, 1713. [NRS.GD124.15.1098/1]

MCGILLIVIE, PATRICK DOW, tenant in Tomnarraw, Lordship of Mar, Aberdeenshire, 1716. [NRS.E646.2.1]

MCGILLIVRAY, JOHN, drummer or piper of the 1st Strathspey Fencible Regiment, 1793. [NRS.GD248.463.1]

MCGREGOR, ALEXANDER, a taxpayer in Glen Muick, 1799. [ACA]

MCGREGOR, CALUM, in Inverenzie, Glencairn, Lordship of Mar, Aberdeenshire, 1716. [NRS.E646.2.1]

MCGREGOR, JAMES, factor on the Urquhart and Strathspey estates, accounts, 1777-1778. [NRS.GD248.235.8]; factor on the Strathspey estate, 1785-1786. [NRS.GD248.1.2]

MCGREGOR, JAMES, a taxpayer in Coldrach, Crathie, 1799. [ACA]

MCGRIGOR, JAMES, born 1769, farmer at Marywell of Birse, died 1806, husband of Margaret Frost. [Birse gravestone, Aberdeenshire]

MCGRUER, GRUER, Sergeant of the 1st Strathspey Fencible Regiment, 1793. [NRS.GD248.463.1]

MACHARDIE, ALEXANDER, tenant in Glenclumry, Lordship of Mar, Aberdeenshire, 1716. [NRS.E646.2.1]

MCHARDIE, BARBARA, spouse of John Lindsay of Lethnot, Angus, a sasine, 1726. [NRS.RS35.XIV.93]

MCHARDIE, CHARLES, in Wester Micras, Tullich, Lordship of Mar, Aberdeenshire, 1716. [NRS.E646.2.1]

MCHARDY, CHARLES, born 1746, minister at Crathie for 34 years, died 1822, spouse Clementina Forbes, born 1755, died 1822. [Crathie gravestone, Aberdeenshire]; a taxpayer in Crathie, 1799. [ACA]

MACHARDIE, DAVID, aboard HMS Nonsuch at Sheerness, son of John McHardie of Crathie, Aberdeenshire, a letter dated 1709. [NRS.GD132.234]

MACHARDIE, FINLAY, of Daldowie, Aberdeenshire, a contract of Wadset, 1713. [NRS.CS238.S.2.45]

SCOTTISH HIGHLANDERS, 1725-1775; GRAMPIAN HIGHLANDS, II

MCHARDIE, FINDLAY, in Deldounie, Tullich, Lordship of Mar, Aberdeenshire, 1716. [NRS.E646.2.1]

MCHARDY, FINDLAY, a taxpayer in Inver, Crathie, 1799. [ACA]

MCHARDIE, ..., of Crathie, in the parish of Crathie, Lordship of Mar, 1716. [NRS.E646.2.2]

MACHIR, DAVID, miller at the Mill of Inverskandy, husband of Margaret Taylor born 1703, died 1751. [Edzell gravestone, Angus]

MCINNES, JOHN, minister at Crathie, Aberdeenshire, a testicate, 1720. [NRS.GD95.14.15]

MCINNIS, JOHN, in Clachnocter, died 1743, father of Robert. [Glen Isla gravestone, Angus]

MCINTOSH, ALEXANDER, in Geillswall, Glen Isla, Angus, his widow Marion Ewen, testament, 1714, Comm. Brechin. [NRS]

MCINTOSH, CHARLES, Corporal of the 1st Strathspey Fencible Regiment, 1793. [NRS.GD248.463.1]

MACINTOSH, DONALD, tenant in Glenclumry, Lordship of Mar, Aberdeenshire, 1716. [NRS.E646.2.1]

MCKINTOSH, DONALD, tenant in Ardchie, Lordship of Mar, Aberdeenshire, 1716. [NRS.E646.2.1]

MCINTOSH, DONALD, Corporal of the 1st Strathspey Fencible Regiment, 1793. [NRS.GD248.463.1]

MACKINTOSH, JOHN, tenant in Castletoun, Lordship of Mar, Aberdeenshire, 1716. [NRS.E646.2.1/2]

MCKINTOSH, JOHN ROY, tenant in Ardchie, Lordship of Mar, Aberdeenshire, 1716. [NRS.E646.2.1]

MCINTOSH, JOHN, in Lethnot, Angus, 1752. [NRS.CH2.628.1.105]

MCINTOSH, JOHN, drummer or piper of the 1st Strathspey Fencible Regiment, 1793. [NRS.GD248.463.1]

MACKINTOSH, WILLIAM, tenant in Bellachlon, Lordship of Mar, Aberdeenshire, 1716. [NRS.E646.2.1]

MCINTOSH, WILLIAM, in the parish of Kindrochit, Lordship of Mar, Aberdeenshire, 1716. [NRS.E646.2.2]

MACKAY, PETER, born 1670, died 19 April 1742, husband of Jean Clark, born 1684, died 12 July 1744, parents of Robert Mackay. [Kincardine O'Neil gravestone]

MCKAY, PETER, Sergeant of the 1st Strathspey Fencible Regiment, 1793. [NRS.GD248.463.1]

MCKAY, THOMAS, born 1773, farmer in Wester Auldallan, died 1854, husband of Jean Ramsay, born 1789, died 1869. [Lintrathen gravestone, Angus]

MCKENZIE, ALEXANDER, tenant in Dalmore, sub factor of the Castleton of Braemar, Aberdeenshire, a deed, 1704. [NRS.GD124.17.96]

MCKENZIE, ALEXANDER, in the parish of Kindrochit, Lordship of Mar, Aberdeenshire, 1716. [NRS.E646.2.2]

MCKENZIE, COLIN, of Strathcathro, Angus, formerly a merchant in Jamaica, son of Kenneth McKenzie f Dalmore, a sasine, 1763. [NRS.RS35.XX.355]

MCKENZIE, DONALD, Corporal of the 1st Strathspey Fencible Regiment, 1793. [NRS.GD248.463.1]

MCKENZIE, or MCDOUGAL, ELIZABETH, born 1744, died 1821. [Glen Isla gravestone, Angus]

MACKENZIE, GEORGE, factor to the Earl of Aboyne, a deed, 4 March 1752. [NRS.RD4.178/1.257]

MCKENZIE, ISABEL, mother of Alexander Ogilvy, and relict of Thomas Ogilvy of Eastmiln of Glenisla, Angus, a sasine, 1750. [NRS.RS35.XVII.462]

MCKENZIE, KENNETH, of Dalmore, the Earl of Mar's forester at Braemar, Aberdeenshire, a letter, 1712. [NRS.GD124.15.1086]

MACKENZIE, KENNETH, of Dalmore, lands of Kindrocht in the Lordship of Mar, Aberdeenshire, 1716, father of Donald McKenzie. [NRS.E646.2.1/2]

MCKENZIE, ROBERT, born 1748, died at Craigmiky in 1825, husband of Ann Robertson, born 1758, died 1839. [Glen Isla gravestone, Angus]

MACKERREBAR, ALEXANDER, tenant in Cornelairg, Lordship of Mar, Aberdeenshire, 1716. [NRS.E646.2.1]

MACKEY, JAMES, a merchant on the Hill of Bettie, Kincardine O'Neill, cautioner for James Shivas an apprentice baker, 1798. [ACA]

MCNABB, DONALD, tenant in Castletoun, Lordship of Mar, Aberdeenshire, 1716. [NRS.E646.2.1]

MCNICOL, DAVID, in Sturt, brother of James McNicol, portioner of Glenmarkie, Angus, a sasine, 1716. [NRS.RS35.13.140]

MCNICHOL, DONALD, a tack of Bollnayell, for 7 years, 1715. [NRS.GD16.Sec.28.301]

MCNICOL, JAMES, of Glenmarkie, Angus, son of James McNicol portioner thereof, husband of Elspeth Bremner or Badenoch, a sasine, 1716. [NRS.RS35.13.140, etc]

MCNICOL, JAMES, portioner of Glenmarkie, Angus, the elder, father of James McNicol, portioner thereof, husband of Margaret Ogilvie, a sasine, 1716. [NRS.RS34.13.140, etc]

MCNICOLL, JAMES, in Auchenleish, Glen Isla, Angus, testament., 1735, Comm. Brechin. [NRS]

MCNICOL, JAMES, nephew of John McNicol, portioner of Glenmarkie, Angus, a sasine, 1760. [NRS.RS35.19.134]

MCNICOL, JAMES, factor to the Earl of Airlie, in Angus, a letter, 1796. [NRS.GD15.49.19]

MCNICOL, THOMAS, portioner of Glenmarkie, Angus, the elder, a sasine, 1716. [NRS.RS35.13.140]

SCOTTISH HIGHLANDERS, 1725-1775; GRAMPIAN HIGHLANDS, II

MCNICOL, THOMAS, overseer at Kinnordy, Angus, 1770s. [NRS.GD205.box 27/222]

MCNIEL, JOHN, drummer or piper of the 1st Strathspey Fencible Regiment, 1793. [NRS.GD248.463.1]

MCPHERSON, ALEXANDER, Sergeant of the 1st Strathspey Fencible Regiment, 1793. [NRS.GD248.463.1]

MCPHERSON, GEORGE, was served heir to his father John McPherson of Invereshie on 9 January 1750. [NRS.S/H]

MCQUEEN, JAMES, Sergeant of the 1st Strathspey Fencible Regiment, 1793. [NRS.GD248.463.1]

MCROBIE, DUNCAN, in Tarland, Aberdeenshire, was discharged from military service as lame in 1757. [ACA.as.amil.2.17]

MCROBBIE, HARRY, a taxpayer in Bridgefoot, Glen Muick, 1799. [ACA]

MCVEAN, PATRICK, in Ballinluig, a letter, 1750. [NRS.E783.8]

MACHIR, DAVID, miller at the Mill of Inverskandy, Angus, husband of Margaret Taylor born 1703, died 1751. [Edzell gravestone, Angus]

MALCOLM, WILLIAM, a workman in Kingoldrum, Angus, a Jacobite in 1745. [OR.38]

MARR, ISABEL, born 1763, died 4 December 1828. [Banchory Devenick gravestone, Aberdeenshire]

MARR, JOHN, born 1715, died 20 March 1807. [Banchory Devenick gravestone, Aberdeenshire]

MARR, MA., born 1702, daughter of William Marr a smith in Tolovhill, died 15 March 1733. [Banchory Devenick gravestone, Aberdeenshire]

MARR, MARGARET, born 1750, died 22 February 1828, spouse of Robert Lyall. [Banchory Devenick gravestone, Aberdeenshire]

MARSHALL, JAMES, in the Meikle Mill, Kinnordy, Angus, 1755. [NRS.GD205.29.239]

MARTIN, CHARLES, Ravernie Mill, Lintrathen, Angus, testament, 1796, Comm. St Andrews. [NRS]

MARTIN, ISOBEL, a tenant in Newbigging, Lethnot, Angus, 1716. [NRS.E650.4]

MARTIN, WILLIAM, son of John Martin in Kirkton of Nether Banchory, was apprenticed to John Imray a baker in Aberdeen, for 5 years, 19 June 1784. [ACA]

MASSIE, SAMUEL, born 1770, died 20 July 1834. [Kincardine O'Neil gravestone]

MASSON, ANN, born 1766, spouse of James Thomson farmer in Netherruthven, died 3 October 1822. [Coull gravestone, Aberdeenshire]

MATHER, CHARLES, born 1725, a ploughman in Braideston, Airlie, a Jacobite in 1745. [OR.38][P.3.12]

MATHER, DAVID, in Lightie, Navar, Angus, 1714, bill of exchange dated 1722. [NRS.CH2.628.17]

MATHER, DAVID, in Lethnot, Angus, 1758. [NRS.CH2.628.1.186]

MATHER, ISOBEL, relict of John Gordon, tenant in Tullyquhille, Lethnot and Navar, Angus, rent book 1733-1749. [NRS.CH2.628/17]

MATHER, MARGARET, in Newbigging, Lethnot, Angus,1757. [NRS.CH2.628/1/153]

MAUCHIN, JOHN, tenant in Littlebridge, Lochlee, Angus, 1716. [NRS.E650.4]

MAVOR, AGNES, born 1729, died 3 August 1803, wife of Jamrs in the Mains of Kincausie. [Banchory Devenish gravestone]

MAVOR, ALEXANDER, born 1715, tenant in Cobbleboards died 7 March 1807, husband of Agnes Duthie, born 1712, died 8 February 1794. [Banchory Devenick gravestone, Kincardineshire]

MAVOR, ROBERT, born 1756, farmer in Hillhead of Skaterow, died 8 March 1811, husband of Jean Craig, born 1767, died 17 January 1826. [Banchory Devenick gravestone, Kincardineshire]

MEARNS, GEORGE, born 1701, tenant in the Mill of Cammie, died 23 June 1781, husband of Jean Robertson, born 1710, died 18 August 1783, parents of Robert, died an infant, Mary, born 1750, died 8 July 1768, Margaret, born 1740, died in January 1796, John, born 1758, died 1 May 1788, George, born 1744, tenant in Curren, died 15 January 1809, Christian, born 1745, died 6 March 1815, Isobel, born 1749, died in February 1819, and David, born 1740, farmer at the Mill of Cammie, died 6 February 1826. [Strachan gravestone]

MELVIL, ALEXANDER, born 1659, died in September 1736, husband of Mary Mc.....born 1659, died 1738, parents of Robert, John, Alexander, and Jean. [Banchory Ternan gravestone]

MERCER, WILLIAM, was granted the lands of Banchory, Aberdeenshire, in 1765. [NRS.SIG1.142.51]

MESTON, WILLIAM, born 1680 in Midmar, a Jacobite in 1715, died 1745. [JAB.158]

MICHIE, MARJORY, died 1790. [Glen Muick gravestone]

MIDDLETON, JAMES, born 1732, died 25 August 1751. [Coull gravestone, Aberdeenshire]

MIDDLETON, JAMES, born 1743, in Marywell, died 27 February 1823, husband of Helen Imray, born 1754, died 2 April 1824, parents of Charles and James. [Birse gravestone]

MIDDLETON, JOHN, in Middlefoord, husband of Elizabeth Coutts, born 1777, died 1802. [Lochlee gravestone, Angus]

MIDDLETON, JOHN, born 1789, farmer at the Mill of Kincraigie, died 6 January 1859, husband of Helen Farquharson, born 1802, died 14 June 1838. [Coull gravestone]

MIDDLETON, JOHN, born 1720, farmer at the Mains of Kincraigie, died 18 December 1808, husband of Christian Thomson, born 1720, died 20 March 1795, parents of James, born 1746, died 17 October 1811. [Coull gravestone]

MIDDLETON, ROBERT, in Mikle Formestoun, 1758, a letter. [NRS.GD181.191/1]

MIDDLETON, ROBERT, born 1751, farmer in Waulkmill of Corse, died 16 May 1825, husband of Isobel Neil. [Coull gravestone]

MIDDLETON, WILLIAM, born 1707, farmer at the Mill of Coull, Aberdeenshire, died November 1797, husband of Helen Torn, born 1717, died September 1777, parents of George, born 17a38, died March 1807, Elisabeth, born 1744, died July 1765, John, born 1752, died May 1791, and Alexander, born 1751, died April 1820. [Coull gravestone]

MILL, ABRAM, in Balnegaro, Kinnordy, Angus, 1755. [NRS.GD205.29.239]

MILL, DAVID, sometime in Braelaus, Cortachy, Angus, relict Janet Soutar, testament., 1711, Comm. Brechin. [NRS]

MILL, DAVID, in Balnatear, Kinnordy, Angus, 1755. [NRS.GD205.29.239]

MILL, GEORGE, of Muirhouse, Kinnordy, Angus, 1755. [NRS.GD205.29.239]

MILL, JAMES, a ploughman in Newton of Airlie, Angus, a Jacobite in 1745, transported to Maryland in 1747. [OR39][TNA.T1.328]

MILL, JAMES, in the Inch, Kinnordy, Angus, 1755. [NRS.GD205.29.239]

MILL, MAGDALENE, widow of John Scott minister at Lochlee, Angus, testament, 1781, Comm. Brechin. [NRS]

MILL, ROBERT, a ploughman in Reedie, Airlie, a Jacobite in 1745. [OR.39]

MILLAR, GEORGE, a mason in the parish of Menmuir, Angus, a deed, 1719. [NRS.E615.10]

MILLAR, THOMAS, of the Clock Mill, Kinnordy, Angus, 1757. [NRS.GD205.29.239]

MILNE, GEORGE, born 1752, farmer in Coy, died 24 February 1834, husband of Margaret Booth, born 1756, died 7 May 1838. [Banchory Ternan gravestone]

MILN, JANET, tenant in Glen Mark, Lochlee, Angus, 1716. [NRS.E650.4]

MILNE, JOHN, born 1736, died 3 August 1804. [Banchory Ternan gravestone]

MILN, ..., of Fern, Angus, 1770. [NRS.E106.16.5]

MILNE, THOMAS, in Dykehead of Cortachy, Angus, husband of Jean Lindsay, sasine, 1709. [NRS.RS35.12/130]

MILNE, WILLIAM, born 1747, farmer in Cowhillock, died 1816, husband of Susan Kennedy, born 1757, died 1835. [Cortachy gravestone, Angus]

MITCHELL, CHARLES, born 1764, tenant in Ennachie, died 1853, husband of Isabel Henderson, born 1772, died 1801. [Birse gravestone, Aberdeenshire]

MITCHELL, GEORGE, husband of Janet Fairweather, born 1656, died 1736, [Careston gravestone, Angus]

MITCHELL, Mrs, a taxpayer in Pananinch, Glen Muick, 1799. [ACA]

MITCHELL, JAMES, eldest son of John Mitchell, portioner of Easter Derry, and Margaret Ogilvy, second daughter of James Ogilvy of the Miln of Craigs, Angus, marriage contract, 1771. [NRS.GD16.41]

MITCHELL, JOHN, in Lethnot, Angus, 1722. [NRS.CH2.628.17]

MITCHELL, JOHN, in Easter Derry, Glen Isla, Angus, 1770. [NRS.E106.16.5]

MITCHELL, THOMAS, a writer in Cortachy, Angus, a deed, 20December 1751. [NRS.RD4.178/1.176]

MITCHELL, THOMAS, at Craig, Angus, factor to the Earl of Airlie, 1780. [NRS.GD16.Sec.41/973]

MOIR, THOMAS, a taxpayer in Black Hillock, Glenbucket, 1799. [ACA]

MOLISON, JAMES, in Navar, 1726; son of .... Molison and his wife Isobell Mather, tenant in Tillyquhillie, Navar, rent book from 1750 to 1755. Ruling elder of Navar, Angus, in 1752. [NRS.CH2.628/17; 628/1/5]

MOLISON, JAMES, the younger, formerly an elder of Menmuir parish, then in Craigendowy, Lethnot, Angus, 1752. [NRS.CH2.628/1/111]

MOLISON, JOHN, of Ballachie, factor to the Earl of Panmure, born 1712, died 1783, husband of Isabel Wishart, born 1730, died 1792. [Navar gravestone] [NRS.CH2.628/17]

MONRO, JAMES, born 1745, late tenant in Marywell, died 4 February 1827, husband of Ann Hay, born 1746, died 8 March 1805. [Birse gravestone, Aberdeenshire]

MORGAN, ELISABETH, in Tornagalter, Tullich, Lordship of Mar, Aberdeenshire, 1716. [NRS.E646.2.1]

MORRICE, Reverend WILLIAM, born 1727, died 22 January 1809, husband of Helen Paterson, born 1744, died April 1817. [Kincardine O'Neil gravestone, Aberdeenshire]

MORRISON, ANDREW, a merchant in Tomintoul, Moray, 1776. [NRS.GD44.23.33.3]

MORTON, JAMES, born 1780, of the Mill of Aboyne, died 17 August 1858, husband of Margaret Murray, born 1793, died 9 March 1880. [Aboyne gravestone]

MUDIE, THOMAS, a ploughman in Baikie, Airlie, Angus, a Jacobite in 1745. [OR.41]

MUILE, JOHN, a taxpayer in Auchnerran, Glen Muick, 1799. [ACA]

MUIR, FRANCIS, a clerk in Braemar, Aberdeenshire, a letter, 1710. [NRS.GD124.15.974.1]

MURRAY, ALEXANDER, born in Glen Isla dring 1781, a wright of West Wynd, Perth Road, Dundee, died 23 August 1847. [St Peter's burial register, Dundee]

MURRAY, ALEXANDER, born 1704, late in Nigg, died 1 July 1765. [Banchory Devenick gravestone]

MYLES, JAMES, a workman in Kingoldrum, a Jacobite in 1745. [OR.41]

NEAVE, CHARLES, schoolmaster at Faulds of Derry, Glen Isla, and at Folda, Glen Isla, from 1751 to 1753. [SSPCK#84]

NEWTON, ALEXANDER, husband of Elspet Adam born 1677, died in Clintley 1701. [Lintrathen gravestone, Angus]

NICOLL, ALEXANDER, servant to John Nicoll, in Keeny, Lochlee, Angus, testament, 1751, Comm. Breechin. [NRS]

NICOLL, ALEXANDER, born 1701, late in Persie, died 30 December 1764, father of Alexander Nicol, born 1737, died 14 March 1761, grandfather of John Grant, born 1760, died 7 October 1775. [Birse gravestone, Aberdeenshire]

NICOLL, ALEXANDER, servant to John Nicoll, in Keeny, Lochlee Angus, testament, 1751, Comm. Brechin. [NRS]

NICOLL, DAVID, tenant in Nether Cairncross, Lochlee, Angus, 1716. [NRS.E650/4]

NICOLL, DAVID, at Aucheen, Lochlee, Angus, testament, 1799, Comm. Brechin. [NRS]

NICOLL, DONALD, tenant in Drusty, Lochlee, Angus, 1716. [NRS.E650/4]

NICOLL, DONALD, late in Aucheen, Angus, testament, 1799, Comm. Brechin. [NRS]

NICOL, JAMES, in Lethnot, Angus, 1752. [NRS.CH2.628/1/88]

NICOLL, JOHN, tenant in Turnabrain, Lochlee, Angus, 1716. [NRS.E650/4]

SCOTTISH HIGHLANDERS, 1725-1775; GRAMPIAN HIGHLANDS, II

NICOLL, JOHN, tenant in Kinie, Lochlee, Angus, 1716. [NRS.E650/4]

NICOLL, JOHN, tenant in Skellie, Lochlee, Angus, 1716. [NRS.E650/4]

NICOL, WALTER, in Waterhead, Lethnot, Angus, 1743. [NRS.CH2.628/17/10]

NICOLL, WILLIAM, tenant in Boddam, Lochlee, Angus, 1716. [NRS.E650/4]

NICOLSON, JAMES, minister at Nether Banchory, Aberdeenshire, letter, 1749. [NRS.GD105.143]

NICOLSON, ROBERT, tenant, Muirhead of Kinnordie, Angus, 1745. [NRS.GD205.box 26/214]

NIVIE, WILLIAM, born 1730, tenant in the Haugh of Spitalburn, died 1 January 1779. [Strachan gravestone, Kincardineshire]

OGG, JOHN, born 1760, tenant in Bridgend of Aboyne, died 7 March 1843, husband of Margaret Jolly, born 1770, died 25 September 1833. [Aboyne gravestone]

OGILVY, ALEXANDER, in Gleslet, Cortachy, Angus, 1721. [NRS.GD16.Sec.28/330]

OGILVY, ALEXANDER, the younger, in the Braes of Lintrathen, a Jacobite in 1745. [OR.42][P.3.226]

OGILVY, ALEXANDER, in New Mill, Kinnordy, Angus, 1755. [NRS.GD205.29.239]

OGILVIE, ALEXANDER, formerly in the East Milne of Glen Isla, Angus, then a surgeon on the merchant ship Chance, testament, 1771, Comm. Edinburgh. [NRS]; a sasine, 1765. [NRS.RS35.21]

OGILVIE, DAVID, of Clova, Angus, testament, 1726, Comm. Brechin. [NRS]

OGILVY, DAVID, of Clunie, and his wife Elizabeth Fullerton, daughter of the late William Fullerton of that Ilk, a marriage contract, 1705, 1728, 1735. [NRS.GD1.116.444.36; 28/332]

OGILVIE, DAVID, minister at Birse, Aberdeenshire, died 1714. [NRS.S/H]

OGILVY, Sir DAVID, of Clova, Angus, testament, 1738, Comm. Brechin. [NRS]

OGILVY, DAVID, of Pool, Lintrathen, a Jacobite in 1745. [LPR.228][P.3.236]

OGILVY, DAVID, in Clachnabrain, Cortachy, Angus, testament, 1748, Comm. Brechin. [NRS]

OGILVY, DAVID, in Ferter, Glen Isla, testament, 1751, Comm. Brechin. [NRS]

OGILVIE, DAVID, tenant in Tarriebuckle, Cortachy, Angus, test., 1758, Comm. Brechin, husband of Jean Lucas, daughter of John Lucas and his daughter Jean Robie in Longholm, Clova, testament, 1779, Comm. Brechin. [NRS]

OGILVY, DAVID, in Ferter, Glen Isla, Angus, testament, 1751, Comm. Brechin. [NRS]

OGILVY, DAVID, of Ascreavie, Angus, 1763, testament, 1787, Comm. Brechin. [NRS.GD205.box 27/220]

OGILVY, DAVID, of Clunie, and his wife Elizabeth Fullerton, daughter of the late William Fullerton of that Ilk, a marriage contract, 1705, 1728, 1735. [NRS.GD1.116.444.36; 28/332; GD16.Sec.28/332]

OGILVIE, DAVID, minister at Birse, a sasine, 1718. [NRS.RS35.13]

OGILVIE, DAVID, grandson of David the Earl of Airlie, and son of John the Earl thereof, husband of Ann Stewart, sasines, 1779. [NRS.RS35.27.279/360]

OGILVIE, ELIZABETH, daughter of James Ogilvie of Ascrevie, and spouse of Thomas Clephan minister at Kingoldrum, sasines, 1712, [NRS.RS35.12.346/477]

OGILVY, GEORGE, born 1715 son of Reverend George Ogilvy in Kirriemuir, minister at Cortachy, Angus, from 1737 to 1745, then at Menmuir, Angus, to 1773, died 1779, husband of (1) Elizabeth Crawford, (2) Isobel Yeoman, parents of George, James, and Alexander. [F.6.280; F.5.280/408]; sasines, 1765. [NRS.RS35.20.174; RS35.11``

OGILVIE, GEORGE, in Baikie, Airlie, Angus, 1770. [NRS.E106/16/5]

OGILVIE, JAMES, at the mill of Ingon, son of James Ogilvie of Inchewan, a sasine, 1736. [NRS.RS35.15.336]

OGILVIE, JAMES, husband of Elizabeth Grant, in Corrymalice, Braemar, a member of the Aberdeenshire Militia in 1808. [ACA.AS.AMI.6.1.1]

OGILVY, JAMES, in the Mains of Kinnordy, Angus, 1758. [NRS.GD205.29.239]

OGILVY, JAMES, of Ascreavie, born 1759, died 1787. [Kingoldrum gravestone, Angus]

OGILVIE, JAMES, in Craig Mill, Glen Isla, Angus, 1770. [NRS.E106/16/5]

OGILVIE, JOHN, of Queich, minister of Cortachy, Angus, from 1706 to 1724. [F.5.280]

OGILVY, JOHN, of Braeside, Angus, testament, 1719, Comm. Brechin. [NRS]

OGILVY, JOHN, second son of the late David Ogilvy, Earl of Airlie, Angus, and Margaret Ogilvie, eldest daughter of David Ogilvie of Cluny, a marriage contract, 1722. [NRS.GD16.44.17]

OGILVY, Sir JOHN, of Inverquharity, Angus, 1735. [NRS.GD205.box 25/187]; was served heir to his father Sir John Ogilvy of Inverquharity in 1735. [NRS.S/H]; a deed, 22 September 1750. [NRS.RD3.210.543]

OGILVY, JOHN, a farmer in Wester Lethnot, Cortachy, a Jacobite in 1745. [OR.2]

OGILVY, JOHN, born 1748, farmer in Powmire, died 1825, husband of Janet Findlay, born 1758, died 1820. [Cortachy gravestone, Angus]

OGILVY, JOHN, a labourer in Cortachy, a Jacobite in 1745. [P.3.238]

OGILVY, JOHN, born 1714, tenant in Arlots, died 1786, husband of Katherine Ego, parents of Jean and Helen. [Clova gravestone, Angus]

OGILVY, JOHN, born 1714, tenant in the Arlots, died 1786, husband of Katherine Ego. [Clova gravestone, Angus]

OGILVIE, Sir JOHN, of Balnamoon, Angus, a sasine 1756. [NRS.RS35.18.171]

OGILVIE, JOHN, minister at Midmar, cautioner for James Smith an apprentice baker in 1797. [ACA]

OGILVY, MARGARET, eldest daughter of Walter Ogilvy of Clova, Angus, and John, Viscount Arbuthnott, a marriage contract, 1805. [NRS.GD15.44.49]

OGILVIE, PATRICK, of Balfour, his relict Margaret Graham, testament, 1732, Comm. Brechin. [NRS]

OGILVY, THOMAS, of the East Mill of Glen Isla, Angus, testament, 1731, Comm. Brechin. [NRS]

OGILVY, THOMAS, of East Mill, Glen Isla, a Jacobite in 1745, died 1751. [OR.3/143][LPR.226][P.3.240]

OGILVY, WALTER, of Clova, Angus, letters dating from 1751. [NRS.GD16.Sec.34/345]

OGILVIE, WALTER, of Clova, Angus, 1768. [NRS.AD58.312]

OGILVY, WALTER, of Clova, Angus, and Jean Ogilvy, second daughter of Dr John Ogilvy a physician in Forfar, a postnuptial marriage contract, 1781. [NRS.GD16.44.42]

OGILVIE, WALTER, of Clova, Angus, and his wife Jean Ogilvy, daughter of Dr John Ogilvie a physician in Forfar, a divorce, 1798. [NRS.CC8.6.1037]

OGILVY, WILLIAM, at Loch Milne, Angus, 1741. [NRS.GD205.box 26/205]

OGILVIE, WILLIAM, in the Mains of Kinnordy, Angus, 1755. [NRS.GD205.29.239]

OGILVIE, ..., of Coull, Ruthven and Lintrathen, Angus, 1770. [NRS.E106/16/5]

PALMER, ROBERT, a workman in Dalairn, Clova, a Jacobite in 1745. [OR.43]

PATERSON, JOHN, a taxpayer in Abergairn, Glen Muick, 1799. [ACA]

PATERSON, ROBERT, subtenant in Reedfaulds, Lethnot, Angus, testament, 1771, Comm. Brechin. [NRS]

PATON, ANDREW, at the Mill of Cortachy, Angus, testament, 1717, Comm. Brechin. [NRS]

PATON, ANDREW, at the Milton of Cortachy, Angus, testaments, 1744, Comm. Brechin. [NRS]

PATON, JAMES, at Bridgend of Cortachy, Angus, testaments, 1728, 1729, Comm. Brechin. [NRS]

PATON, JAMES, at Milton of Cortachy, Angus, testament, 1744, Comm. Brechin. [NRS]

PEDDIE, JOHN, born 1708, son of John Peddie, a workman in Kinclune, Kingoldrum, Angus, a Jacobite in 1745. [OR.44]

PEIRIE, JAMES, in the Milton of Cortachy, Angus, 1740. [NRS.GD16.Sec.41/946]

PETER, DAVID, elder of Cortachy and Clova, Angus, 1748. [NRS.CH2.561/3/13]

PETER, ROBERT, born 1742, a smith in Pitmudie, Lintrathen, Angus, died 1798, husband of Elspeth Ogilvy. [Lintrathen gravestone]

PETER, WALTER, merchant in Dykehead, Cortachy, Angus, testament, 1791, Comm. Brechin. [NRS]

PETRIE, COLIN, brother of George Petrie of Newton Prema now at the Mill of Gairth in Aberdeenshire, and Isabel Alexander, daughter of Reverend John Alexander minister at Kildrummy, Aberdeenshire, a marriage contract, 1711. [NRS.CH12.23.5]

PHILLIPS, JOHN, born 1744, farmer in East Mill of Glen Isla, Angus, died 1804, husband of Janet Ogilvie, born 1753, died 1826. [Glen Isla gravestone, Angus]

PHILIP, GEORGE, in Kilduthy, father of Christian born 1771, died 25 December 1796, and of William, born 1773, died 19 December 1796. [Banchory Ternan gravestone]

PIRIE, JOHN, son of John Pirie in Arbuthnott, Kincardineshire, educated at Marischal College, Aberdeen, minister at Lochlee, Angus, from 1771 until his death in 1806, husband of Helen Webster, died 1795, parents of Jean, Isabel, John, James, Margaret, Robert, Katherine, and Ann. [F.5.402]

PRESSACK, JANET, in Inverharity, Angus, an inhibition, 1800. [NRS.D1.128.1.xlviii.338]

RAITT, WILLIAM, in Glen Ogilvy, Angus, 1720. [NRS.RS35.13.166]

RAMSAY, Sir ALEXANDER, of Balmain, landowner of Durres in the parish of Strachan in 1771. [NRS.E106.18.3]

RAMSAY, Sir ALEXANDER, was granted a Crown Charter of the lands of Glenesk, Angus, in 1750. [NRS.SIG1.141.59]

RAMSAY, Sir JAMES, in Drumfoggies, Glen Ogilvy, Angus, 1770. [NRS.CH2.628/16/5]

RAMSAY, JANET, in Lethnot, Angus, 1759. [NRS.CH2.628.1.234]

RAMSAY, JOHN, of Kinalty, husband of Mary Ogilvy, father of John etc., disposition, 1779. [NRS.GD16.Sec.41/969]

RAMSAY, PATRICK, of Lethnot, Angus,1736. [NRS.GD16.Sec.41/937; GD16.41.937]

RAMSAY, PATRICK, of Braemunzion, 1750. [NRS.GD16.13.86]

RAMSAY, PETER, of Lethnot, a deed, 19 May 1750. [NRS.RD2.167.363]

RAMSAY, THOMAS, born 1768, second son of Sir Alexander Ramsay of Balmain and his wife Elizabeth Bannerman, a Captain in the British Army, fought in the Peninsula War and at Waterloo, died 1857. [Banchory-Ternan gravestone, Kincardineshire]

RAMSAY, WILLIAM, born in Moray around 1755, graduated MA from King's College, Aberdeen, in 1775, minister of Cortachy, Angus, from 1795 to his death in 1818, husband of Barbara Grant, parents of Robert, Barbara, William, John, and Jane Ogilvy. [F.5.281]

RANNIE, ARTHUR, born 1740, died 12 January 1836, husband of Ann Gibbon, born 1756, died 20 February 1836. [Glenbuchat gravestone, Aberdeenshire]

RANNIE, JOHN, born 1738, a merchant in Easter Bucket, died 4 June 1767. [Glenbuchat gravestone, Aberdeenshire]

RATTRAY, ANDREW, born 1744, died at East Mill in 1804, husband of Janet Robertson, born 1749, died 1812. [Glen Isla gravestone, Angus]

RATTRAY, FRANCIS, of Kirkhillocks, Kirkton of Glen Isla, Angus, a sasine, 1781. [NRS.RS35.19]

RATTRAY, JAMES, of Kirkhillocks, born 1771, died 1853, husband of Johan Rattray, born 1781, died 1813. [Glen Isla gravestone, Angus]

RATTRAY, JOHN, in the parish of Kindrochit, Lordship of Mar, Aberdeenshire, 1716. [NRS.E646.2.2]

RAWER, ALEXANDER, born 1750, farmer in Easter Powlair, died 1829, husband of Mary Ross, born 1758, died 1823. [Birse gravestone, Aberdeenshire]

REA, CHARLES, in Caldam, Kinnordy, Angus, 1755. [NRS.GD205.29.239]

REACH, JOHN, born 1736, late in Loinmuie, died 1 February 1801, husband of Jean Davidson, born 1754, died 11 February 1844. [Glen Muick gravestone]

REID, ANDREW, born 1777, died 9 February 1851. [Kincardine O'Neil gravestone]

REID, ARCHIBALD, a taxpayer in Bellimore, Glenbucket, 1799. [ACA]

REID, ARCHIBALD, a taxpayer in Kirkton, Glenbucket, 1799. [ACA]

REID, DAVID, in Auchrannie, Glen Isla, Angus, 1770. [NRS.E106/16/5]

REID, JAMES, a taxpayer in Belhenny, Glen Muick, 1799. [ACA]

REID, JEAN, born 1702, died 24 May 1782. [Glenbuchat gravestone, Aberdeenshire]

REID, JOHN, a taxpayer in Milltown, Glenbucket, 1799. [ACA]

REID, KATHERINE, wife of John Lumsden in Mill of Coull, was served heir to her father Robert Reid in Ballbrydie on 5 July 1760. [NRS.S/H]

REID, PETER, a taxpayer in Bellimore, Glenbucket, 1799. [ACA]

REID, ROBERT, born 1776, farmer in Cromore, died 9 April 1855, husband of Isabella Adam, born 1783, died at Arbeadie Place, Banchory Ternan, on 11 October 1850. [Kincardine O'Neil gravestone]

REID, THOMAS, born 1657, late in Pitenkirie, died 1733, husband of Agnes Ferguson, born 1658, died 1728. [Banchory Ternan gravestone, Kincardineshire]

REID, WILLIAM, of Auchmillan, Aberdeenshire, and Barbara Alexander, daughter of John Alexander minister at Kildrummy, Aberdeenshire, a marriage contract, 1715. [NRS.CH12.23.6]

REID, WILLIAM, a taxpayer in Bellabeg, Glen Muick, 1799. [ACA]

REITH, JAMES, born 1762, farmer at Catterloch, died 1836, husband of Isabella Strachan, born 1771, died 1821. [Banchory-Ternan gravestone, Kincardineshire]

RIACH, JOHN, born 1736, died at Nethermill of Towie, 25 December 1800, husband of Margaret Forbes, born 1724, died 25 November 1823, parents of May, [1766-1829], and Margaret, [1767-1832]. [Migvie gravestone, Aberdeenshire]

RIDDLE, ALEXANDER, born 1759 in Achindore, Aberdeenshire, a blacksmith, enlisted in the Aberdeenshire Fencibles in 1778. [NRS.GD44.47.11]

RIDLER, JANET, spouse to Alexander Burnet in Upper Banchory, testament, 1733, Comm. Aberdeen. [NRS]

RIDLER, THOMAS, born 1684, tenant in Drumshalach, died 5 March 1750, husband of Janet Tyler, born 1686, died 15 April 1761, parents of William Ridler, born 1713, died 16 August 1775. [Banchory Ternan gravestone]

ROBERTSON, ALEXANDER, in the parish of Kindrochit, Lordship of Mar, Aberdeenshire, 1716. [NRS.E646.2.2]

ROBERTSON, ALEXANDER, tenant in Castletoun, Lordship of Mar, Aberdeenshire, 1716. [NRS.E646.2.1]

ROBERTSON, ALEXANDER, born 1760 in Cabrach, Aberdeenshire, a laborer, enlisted in the Aberdeenshire Fencibles in 1778. [NRS.GD44.47.11]

ROBERTSON, ALEXANDER, Sergeant of the 1st Strathspey Fencible Regiment, 1793. [NRS.GD248.463.1]

ROBERTSON, CHARLES, born 1753, miller at the Mill of Balmoral, died 26 March 1812. [Glen Muick gravestone]

ROBERTSON, CHARLES, and ROBERT, in Newton of Glenisla, Angus, a tack, 1717. [NRS.GD16.Sec.28.311]

ROBERTSON, DONALD, late in Tulloch, Glen Isla, Angus, testament., 1770, Comm. Brechin. [NRS]

ROBERTSON, DUNCAN, tenant in Castletoun, Lordship of Mar, Aberdeenshire, 1716. [NRS.E646.2.1]

ROBERTSON, DUNCAN, in the parish of Kindrochit, Lordship of Mar, Aberdeenshire, 1716. [NRS.E646.2.2]

ROBERTSON, HENRY, Corporal of the 1st Strathspey Fencible Regiment, 1793. [NRS.GD248.463.1]

ROBERTSON, ISAAC, a fisherman on the River Dee, a letter, 1758. [NRS.GD181.192/20]

ROBERTSON, ISAAC, a taxpayer in Dee Castle, Glen Muick, 1799. [ACA]

ROBERTSON, JAMES, MA, minister of Menmuir, Angus, from 1701 to 1709. [F.5.408]

ROBERTSON, JAMES, was granted the lands of Banchory, Aberdeenshire, in 1765. [NRS.SIG1.142.51]

ROBERTSON, JAMES, born 1751, miller at Mill of Stiren, died 21 May 1808. Husband of Christian, born 1751, died 21 January 1800. [Glen Muick gravestone]

ROBERTSON, JAMES, a taxpayer in Ballaterach, Glen Muick, 1799. [ACA]

ROBERTSON, JEAN, born 1671, died 30 March 1741, spouse of Thomas Couts a shoemaker in Lochtoun of Leys. [Banchory Ternan gravestone]

ROBERTSON, JOHN, minister at Glen Muick and Tullich, Aberdeenshire, a letter, 1713. [NRS.GD124.15.1096/1]; died 11 July 1718. [Glen Muick gravestone]

ROBERTSON, WILLIAM, tenant in Castletoun, Lordship of Mar, Aberdeenshire, 1716. [NRS.E646.2.1/2]

ROBERTSON, WILLIAM, born 1743 in Cabrach, Aberdeenshire, a laborer, enlisted in the Aberdeenshire Fencibles in 1778. [NRS.GD44.47.11]

ROBB, JAMES, of Migby, Kinnordy, Angus, 1755. [NRS.GD205.29.239]

ROBBIE, ALEXANDER, tenant in Middleford, Lochlee, Angus, 1716. [NRS.E650/4]

ROBIE, ALEXANDER, born 1762, tenant in the Mill of Inverscandly, died 1830, husband of Ann Lindsay, born 1770, died 1845. [Edzell gravestone, Angus]

ROBIE, DONALD, born 1762, farmer in Marywell, died 9 September 1829, husband of Janet Coutts, born 1771, died 1808. [Birse gravestone, Aberdeenshire]

ROBIE, FRANCIS, born 1783, gamekeeper at Finzean, died 26 December 1861. [Birse gravestone]

ROBBIE, JOHN, born 1772, in Tillyfruskie, died 1857, husband of Elizabeth Ross, born 1779, died 1857. [Birse gravestone, Aberdeenshire]

ROBBIE, WILLIAM, tenant in Tillygarmonth, husband of [1] Elizabeth Smith, born 1717, died 1764, parents of Francis, Margaret, Donald, William, Isobell and Alexander, [2] Christian Mollison, parents of Anne, Janet, James, and John. [Birse gravestone, Aberdeenshire]

RODGER, DAVID, schoolmaster at Glen Prosen, Angus, from 1740 to 1749. [SSPCK#90]

RONALD, JAMES, and his spouse Agnes Mitchell, in Clova, Aberdeenshire, an inhibition, 1794. [NRS.D1.128.1.lxxvi.528]

ROSE, DAVID, born 1695, an Episcopal clergyman at Lethnot and Lochlee, Angus, died 1758, husband of Margaret Rose, born 1705, died 1785. [NRS.CH2.628/17]

ROSS, ALEXANDER, tenant in Glen Tenant, Lochlee, Angus, 1716. [NRS.E650/4]

ROSS, ALEXANDER, schoolmaster at Lochlee, husband of Jean Cattenach, born 1702, died 1779. [Lochlee gravestone, Angus]

ROSS, DONALD, [1], drummer or piper of the 1st Strathspey Fencible Regiment, 1793. [NRS.GD248.463.1]

ROSS, DONALD, [2], drummer or piper of the 1st Strathspey Fencible Regiment, 1793. [NRS.GD248.463.1]

ROSS, DONALD, [1], Sergeant of the 1st Strathspey Fencible Regiment, 1793. [NRS.GD248.463.1]

ROSS, DONALD, [2], Sergeant of the 1st Strathspey Fencible Regiment, 1793. [NRS.GD248.463.1]

ROSS, HUGH, in Balfour of Durris, Kincardineshire, an inhibition, 1790. [NRS.D1.128.1.v.105]

ROSS, JEAN, in Lethnot, Angus, 1749. [NRS.CH2.628/1]

ROSS, ISABEL, born 1697, died 1749, spouse to John Stuart in the Forest of Birse. [Birse gravestone, Aberdeenshire]

ROSS, JOHN, born 1757, farmer in Dykehead, Aboyne, died 16 November 1844, husband of Sarah Calder, born 1775, died 25 June 1848. [Coull gravestone]

ROSS, WILLIAM, in Brownie, Durris, testament, 14 June 1784, Comm. Aberdeen. [NRS]

ROSS, THOMAS, born 12 September 1789, farmer in the Mins of Findrack, died 24 January 1862. [Kincardiine O'Neil gravestone]

ROSS, WILLIAM, born 1716 in Coull, died 1779, husband of Elspet Tawse, born 1710, died 1785, parents of Alexander. [Birse gravestone, Aberdeenshire]

ROSS, WILLIAM, born 1764, farmer at Bardshillock, died 23 May 1823. [Banchory Ternan gravestone]

ROSS, WILLIAM, born 1763, a vintner in Aberdeen, died 1830, husband of Elizabeth Ross, born 1765, died 1806. [Birse gravestone, Aberdeenshire]

ROSS, WILLIAM, born 1767, farmer at Bardshillock, died 1823, husband of Helen. [Banchory Ternan gravestone, Kincardineshire]

ROUST, ANDREW, born 1760, tenant in Brucklebogg, died 1835, husband of Elisabeth Smith, born 1778, died 1824. [Banchory Ternan gravestone, Kincardineshire]

ROUST, WILLIAM, born 1716, farmer in the Mill of Easter Beilty, died 1769, husband of Elspat Burnet, born 1722, died 1797, parents of Jean, and Euphemia. [Banchory Ternan gravestone, Kincardineshire]

ROW, JOHN, born in Leslie, graduated MA from St Andrews in 1697, minister from 1718 to 1723, at Navar from 1718 to 1723, then at Lethnot and Navar, Angus, died 1745, husband of Elizabeth Young, died 1746, tests., 1746, Comm. Brechin. [Lethnot gravestone, Angus] [NRS.SC20.36/8][F.5.399]

SALMOND, JOHN, tenant in Bellachlon, Lordship of Mar, Aberdeenshire, 1716. [NRS.E646.2.1]

SAMSON, ANDREW, in Glen Isla, a Jacobite in 1745. [P.3.298]

SAMSON, WILLIAM, a workman in Lintrathen, Angus, a Jacobite in 1745. [OR.10]

SANGSTER, GEORGE, born 1681, schoolmaster at Upper Banchory, a deed, 1737. [ACA.APB.3]

SCADD, ALEXANDER, in Tullicairn, dead by 1721. [NRS.GD181.201/8]

SCOTT, JAMES, born 1707, in Waterstoun Mill, died 1794. [Fern gravestone, Angus]

SCOTT, JOHN, minister at Lochlee, Angus, from 1731 to his death in 1733, husband of Magdalen Milne died 1781, sasines,

1736, testaments, 1749, 1781, Comm. Brechin.
[NRS.RS35.15/392, etc]

SCROGGIE, GEORGE, tenant of Durris, Kincardineshire, 1733.
[NRS.CS271.40796]

SHAND, ROBERT, a distiller in Durris, Kincardineshire, sederunt book, 1781. [NRS.CS96.4448]

SHANKS, JOHN, tenant in Arsellach, Lochlee, 1716.
[NRS.E650.4]

SHANK, MARTIN, minister at Upper Banchory, testament, 24 September 1747, Comm. Aberdeen. [NRS]

SHAW, DONALD, portioner of Crochinard, lands of Crathie in the Lordship of Mar, Aberdeenshire, 1716. [NRS.E646.2.1]

SHAW, DUNCAN, and the heirs of John McHardie, for the lands of Crathie and Cratenaird, Aberdeenshire, 1716. [NRS.E646.2.1]

SHAW, DUNCAN, of Daldownie, and in Cortachy, Angus, sasine, 1766. [NRS.RS35.21/268]

SHAW, DUNCAN, in Milton of Cortachy, Angus, testaments, 1779, 1796, Comm. Brechin. [NRS]

SHAW, DUNCAN, in Balloach of Glen Isla, Angus, testament, 1782, Comm. Brechin. [NRS]

SHAW, JAMES, of Crathienard, in the parish of Crathie, Lordship of Mar, Aberdeenshire, 1716. [NRS.E646.2.2]

SHAW, JAMES, of Crathie, a contract of Wadset, 1713.
[NRS.CS238.S.2.45]

SHAW, JAMES, of Daldowie, son of the late Duncan Shaw of Crathie, Aberdeenshire, 1734. [NRS.GD124.7.74]

SHAW, JOHN, tenant in Migvie, Lochlee, Angus, 1716.
[NRS.E650/4]

SHAW, JOHN, tenant in Migvie, Lochlee, Angus, 1716.
[NRS.E650/4]

SHAW, JOHN, Corporal of the 1st Strathspey Fencible Regiment, 1793. [NRS.GD248.463.1]

SHAW, MARJORY, in the parish of Kindrochit, Lordship of Mar, Aberdeenshire, 1716. [NRS.E646.2.2]

SHAW, MARJORY, relict of John Lyon, sometime in Tombay of Glenshee, a deed, 17... [NRS.GD16.Sec.42.745]

SHAW, WILLIAM, a farmer in Drumfin, Glen Isla, a Jacobite in 1745, died 1790, [OR3/157]

SHAW, WILLIAM, born 27 December 1757 in Inveraven, died 19 December 1833 in Bellfield, Banchory Ternan. [Banchory Ternan gravestone]

SHEPHERD, GEORGE, son of John Shepherd in Invermarkie, Glass, Aberdeenshire, educated at Marischal College, Aberdeen, MA 1709, minister at Aboyne and Glentanar, Aberdeenshire, from 1716 to his death in 1752, married Katherine Alexander,1717, parents of John, Isabel, Joseph, and Elizabeth. [F.6.78]; testament, 26 November 1754, Comm. Aberdeen. [NRS]

SHERRAR, HUGH, born 1748, a farmer in Footie, died 27 January 1825, husband of Jean Cromar. [Kincardine O'Neil gravestone]

SIME, JAMES, a gardener in Cortachy, 1728, husband of Katherine Leuchars who died in 1749. [NRS.GD205.box 21/21] [Cortachy gravestone, Angus]

SINCLAIR, FRANCIS, born 1734, a farmer in Dubbieloare, died June 1800. [Kincardine O'Neil gravestone]

SIVEWRIGHT, JAMES, born 1750 in Rhynie, Aberdeenshire, a laborer, enlisted in the Aberdeenshire Fencibles in 1778. [NRS.GD44.47.11]

SIVEWRIGHT, ROBERT, born 1733, famer in the Haugh of Strachan, died 23 November 1813, husband of Isabel Imray. [Strachan gravestone]

SMART, AGNES, in Nathie, Lethnot, 1757. [NRS.CH2.628/1/170]

SMART, ALEXANDER, and his wife Ann Low, in Lethnot, 1768. [NRS.CH2.628/1/257]

SMART, ANDREW, in Lethnot, 1722; tenant in Achurie, died 1740, husband of Jean Milne, born 1680, died 1748, parents of Andrew, David, Thomas, John, and Alexander.
[NRS.CH2.628/17; E650/4] [Lethnot gravestone]

SMART, DAVID, born 1700, in Polburn, died 1753, spouse Ann Tosh, born 1701, died 1759, parents of Margaret, David, Andrew, John, Isabel, Alexander, Agnes, Andrew, Ann, Joseph, Margaret, Thomas, and Jean. [Lethnot gravestone, Angus]
SMART, DAVID, tenant in Green Burn, husband of Janet Christison, born 1704, died 1749, parents of Anna, John, David, Mary, and Jean. [Edzell gravestone, Angus]

SMART, DAVID, packman in Lethnot, Angus, testament, 1697, Comm. Brechin. [NRS]

SMART, DAVID, born 1706, a ploughman in Drumcairn and in Dykehead of Drumcairn 44 years, died 1770, wife Katherine Tulloa. [Lethnot gravestone, Angus]

SMART, DAVID, born 1706, tenant of Townhead, died 1771, husband of (1) Ann Alexander, parents of David, Thomas, and Margaret, and (2) Agnes Grant, parents of John, Ann, and Mary. [Lethnot gravestone]

SMART, JOHN, tenant in Ardgoill, Lethnot, 1716. [NRS.E650/4]

SMART, WILLIAM, born 1770, in Wester Inchbrathy, Angus, died 1805, husband of Elspet Low. [Glen Prosen gravestone, Angus]

SMITH, ALEXANDER, a hammerman in the parish of Menmuir, a deed, 1719. [NRS.E615.10]

SMITH, ALEXANDER, born 1722, in Clachinturn, died 1793. [Crathie gravestone]

SMITH, ALEXANDER, and his wife Elspet Low, in Lethnot, 1768. [NRS.CH2.628/1/256]

SMITH, ALEXANDER, born 1751, tenant in Candies Hill, died 11 December 1822, husband of Agnes Douglas, born 1755, died 13 November 1818, parents of John Smith, born 1777, farmer in Candies Hill, died 7 June 1858. [Banchory Ternan gravestone]

SMITH, DONALD, in Strath Girnick, died 1783, spouse Euphan Coutts. [Crathie gravestone]

SMITH, DONALD, in Weard Head, died 1805. [Glen Muick gravestone]

SMITH, JAMES, of Muirhouse, Kinnordy, Angus, 1755. [NRS.GD205.29.239]

SMITH, JAMES, born 1754 in Rhynie, Aberdeenshire, a labourer, enlisted in the Aberdeenshire Fencibles in 1778. [NRS.GD44.47.11]

SMITH, JAMES, in the Brae of Airlie, Angus, an inhibition, 1792. [NRS.D1.128.1.xlviii.163]

SMITH, JOHN, born 1754, farmer in Borrowston, died 29 March 1822, husband of Jean Merchant, born 1759, died 24 August 1841. [Kincardine O'Neil gravestone]

SMITH, JOHN, born 1717, in Clachenturn, died 1789. [Crathie gravestone, Aberdeenshire]

SMITH, JOHN, born 1734, tenant in Dalfooper, died 1813, husband of Isabella Molleson, born 1745, died 1833. [Edzell gravestone, Angus]

SMITH, JOHN, drummer or piper of the 1st Strathspey Fencible Regiment, 1793. [NRS.GD248.463.1]

SMITH, JOSEPH, born 1749, minister in Birse, died 7 September 1831, husband of Barbara Reid, born 1759, did 12 December 1825. [Birse gravestone]

SMITH, PETER, died in 1790, his wife Janet Watt died in 1796. [Glen Muick gravestone]

SMITH, ROBERT, husband of Isobel Adam, born 1713, died 1748. [Airlie gravestone, Angus]

SMITH, WILLIAM, tenant in Tarfside, Lochlee, 1716. [NRS.E650/4]

SMITH, ..., of Peel, Lintrathen, 1770. [NRS.E106/16/5]

SMITH, WILLIAM, husband of Margaret Buck, in Nether Banchory, a member of the Aberdeenshire Militia in 1805. [ACA.AS.AMI.6.1.1]

SPALDEN, DAVID, in the Mains of Cortachy, Angus, a tack, 1715. [NRS.GD16.Sec.28.303]

SPALDING, JOHN, in Burnside, Glen Isla, 1770. [NRS.E106/16/5]

SPEED, ROBERT, reader at Lochlee, 1715; tenant in Kirkton of Lochlee, 1716. [NRS.RD4.116.59; E650/4]

SPEED, WILLIAM, tenant in Blairno, Lethnot and Navar, Angus, 1742-1783. [NRS.CH2.628/17]

SPENCE, JOHN, servant to the laird of Invercauld, testament, 5 February 1741, Comm. Aberdeen. [NRS]

SPENCE, Reverend, a taxpayer in Glenbucket, 1799. [ACA]

STABLES, HELEN and CHRISTIAN, in Charleston of Aboyne, testament, 4 March 1755, Comm. Aberdeen. [NRS]

STEEL, THOMAS, in Inchaen, Lintrathen, Angus, died 1746, his wife died in 1729. [Lintrathen gravestone]

STELLAS, ALEXANDER, born 1696, died 9 September 1766, husband of Jean Gillespie, born 1708, died 5 November 1774, parents of Alexander, born 1739, died 6 April 1806, Jean, and Janet. [Banchory Ternan gravestone]

STEPHEN, JAMES, born 1733, farmer at Milton of Brachley, died 24 December 1788, husband of Jannet Ewen, born 1743, died 8 October 1821. [Glen Muick gravestone]

STEVENSON, ANN, born 1736, died 14 February 1768, wife of Alexander Murray a mariner in Aberdeen. [Banchory Devenick gravestone]

STEWART, ALEXANDER, tacksman of Auchvockie in Strathspey, a deed, 1750. [NRS.CC2.2.42.2]

STEWART, ALEXANDER, vintner in Braehead of Kirkton of Aberlour, Moray, an inhibition, 1793. [NRS.D1.128.1.vii.282]

STEWART, ANDREW, in the parish of Kindrochit, Lordship of Mar, Aberdeenshire, 1716. [NRS.E646.2.2]

STEWART, ANDREW BAIN, tenant in Glenclumry, Lordship of Mr, Aberdeenshire, 1716. [NRS.E646.2.1]

STEWART, CHARLES, Corporal of the 1st Strathspey Fencible Regiment, 1793. [NRS.GD248.463.1]

STEWART, DONALD, in the parish of Kindrochit, Lordship of Mar, Aberdeenshire, 1716. [NRS.E646.2.2]

STEWART, DONALD BAIN, tenant in Cornelairg, Lordship of Mar, Aberdeenshire, 1716. [NRS.E646.2.1]

STEWART, ELISABETH, born 1770, died 9 January 1814, wife of John Sector. [Birse gravestone]

STEWART, GEORGE, Corporal of the 1st Strathspey Fencible Regiment, 1793. [NRS.GD248.463.1]

STEWART, HELEN, died 1777. [Glen Muick gravestone]

STEWART, JAMES, born 1718, merchant in Torragaiter, died 1773. [Crathie gravestone]

STEWART, JAMES, born 1722, died 1797, husband of Christiana Buchan. [Cortachy gravestone, Angus]

STEWART, JAMES, died 1787, husband of Elizabeth Blair. [Glen Muick gravestone]

STEWART, JOHN, in Crofts of Glenbucket, testament, 20 November 1778, Comm. Aberdeen. [NRS]

STEWART, JOHN, in Alrick, Glen Isla, testament, 1760, Comm. Brechin. [NRS]

STEWART, JOHN, died 1794. [Glen Muick gravestone]

STEWART, JOHN, at Folda, husband of Christian Charles, born 1746, died 1818. [Glen Isla gravestone, Angus]

STEWART, JOHN, born 1754, died 1815. [Airlie gravestone, Angus]

STEWART, JOHN, a taxpayer in Tullich, Glen Muick, 1799. [ACA]

STEWART, MARGARET, relict of John Stewart minister of Kilmanivaig, deceased, and their children Robert and Ann, deed, 1750. [NRS.CC2.2.42.2]

STEWART, ROBERT, factor on the Mar estate, Aberdeenshire, 1716. [NRS.E645.56]

STEWART, ROBERT, died 1788. [Glen Muick gravestone]

STEWART, THOMAS JOHN, a surgeon inKincardine O'Neil, testament, 1797, Comm. Aberdeen. [NRS]

STEWART, WALTER, died 1776. [Glen Muick gravestone]

STEWART, Mr, a taxpayer in Allanquick, Crathie, 1799. [ACA]

STORMONTH, ELIZABETH, daughter of John Stewart, in Acharn, Clova, testament, 1752, Comm. Brechin. [NRS]

STORMONTH, JOHN, in Acharn, Clova, deceased, father of Elizabeth, testament, 1752, Comm. Brechin. [NRS]

STRACHAN, ALEXANDER, was granted a Crown Charter of the lands of Glenesk, Angus, in 1704. [NRS.SIG1.151.44]

STRACHAN, ALEXANDER, petitioned for the roup of Edzell, Angus, 1711. [NRS.CS236.S.1.44]

STRACHAN, ALEXANDER, of Glenkindly, resigned the lands of Glenkindly in favour of Patrick Strachan of Glenkindly in 1710. [NRS.GD124.1.398]

STRACHAN, ALEXANDER, of Dalhakie, 1738. [NRS.CS313.1034]

STRACHAN, ARTHUR, in Overangustown, a tack, 1800. [NRS.GD105.557]

STRACHAN, CHRISTIAN, daughter of Sir Patrick Strachan of Glenkindy, an adjudication, 1732. [NRS.CS181.7470]

STRACHAN, ELIZABETH, daughter of Sir Patrick Strachan of Glenkindy, an adjudication, 1732. [NRS.CS181.7470]

STRACHAN, or RAMSAY, HUGH, a Catholic priest in Auchindryan, Braemar, 1725. [NRAS.771.811]

STRACHAN, HUGH, born 1785, died 17 March 1861, husband of Mary Kerr. [Birse gravestone]

STRACHAN, JOHN, born 1696, in Campfield, died 1777, husband of Janet Still. [Kincardine O'Neil gravestone]

STRACHAN, PATRICK, was granted a Crown Charter of the lands of Glen Kindy, in 1716. [NRS.SIG1.153.13]; the Surveyor General of the Forfeited Estates in 1717. [NRS.E608]

STRACHAN, PETER, born 1736, in Pitmeddan, died 12 May 1800, husband of Euphemia Mitchel, born 1737, died 26 November 1800. [Kincardine O'Neil gravestone]

STUART, ALEXANDER, in Waterhead, Lethnot, Angus, 1743. [NRS.CH2.628/17/10]

STUART, ALEXANDER, in Allanacraig, and his sons John and Nathaniel, a contract, 1731. [NRS.GD181.191/6]

STUART, ALEXANDER, a gardener in Cookston, Airlie, a Jacobite in 1745. [OR.10]

STUART, JAMES, a workman in Kingoldrum, Angus, a Jacobite in 1745. [OR.51]

STUART, WILLIAM, of Acholy, dead by 1729. [NRS.GD181.231]

STUART, WILLIAM, born 1745, farmer in the Mains of Durris, died 15 December 1806, husband of Elizabeth Anderson, born 1748, died 1 December 1820. [Strachan gravestone]

SUTHERLAND, ROBERT, drummer or piper of the 1st Strathspey Fencible Regiment, 1793. [NRS.GD248.463.1]

SUTHERLAND, JOHN, in Fettercairn, Kincardineshire, 1790s. [NRS.E326.7.4.94]

SYMMER, GEORGE, in Navar, 1726. [NRS.CH2.628/17]

SYMMER, JAMES, in Dubton, Fern, Angus, testament, 1741, Comm. Brechin. [NRS]

SYMON, CHARLES, schoolmaster in Glen Esk, 1766. [SSPCK#101]

SYMON, JAMES, portioner of Lausy, Lordship of Mar, Aberdeenshire, 1716. [NRS.E646.2.2]

SYMON, JOSEPH, a workman at Cortachy, Angus, a roup roll, 1785. [NRS.GD16.43.45]

SYMON, CHARLES, schoolmaster in Glen Esk, 1766. [SSPCK#101]

SYMONDS, MURDOCH, a taxpayer in Mains of Monaltrie, Crathie, 1799. [ACA]

SYMSON, ALEXANDER, graduated MA from King's College, Aberdeen, 1666, minister of Navar from 1670 to his death in 1707, husband of Margaret Carnegie. [F.5.401]

SYMSON, DONALD, portioner of Losie, Crathie, Lordship of Mar, Aberdeenshire, 1716. [NRS.E646.2.1]

SYMSON, JAMES, portioner of Losie, Crathie, Lordship of Mar, Aberdeenshire, 1716. [NRS.E646.2.1]

TAWSE, WILLIAM, born 1767, died 31 October 1858, husband of Elizabeth McKenzie born 1779, died 20 January 1848, parents of William Tawse in Guelph, Canada. [Birse gravestone]

TAYLOR, DAVID, born 1688, died at Netherton of Melgund 1746. [Fern MI]

TAYLOR or CARNEGIE, ELSPETH, born 1757, died 1795. [Fern gravestone, Angus]

TAYLOR, JOHN, graduated MA from King's College, Aberdeen, in 1765, minister of Lethnot and Navar, Angus, from 1775 to his death in 1808, husband of Isabel Pirie, parents of Helen, Ann, Alexander, John, Robert, David, Margaret, and Katherine. [F.5.399]

TAYLOR, ROBERT, of Auchinbannald, papers, 1681-1718. [NRS.E646.70]

THOM, ALEXANDER, born 1723, died in October 1749. [Birse gravestone, Aberdeenshire]

THOM, GEORGE, a workman in Lintrathan, a Jacobite in 1745. [OR.52]

THOM, JOHN, in Park Inn, Drumoak, born 1789, died 9 June 1862, husband of Christian Taylor, born 1788, died 2 January 1858. [Banchory Tiernan gravestone]

THOMSON, ALEXANDER, was granted the lands of Banchory in 1744. [NRS.SI1.164.10]

THOMSON, ISABEL, tenant in Westbank, Lochlee, 1716. [NRS.E650/4]

THOMSON, JAMES, minister at Edzell, Angus, testament, 1729, Comm. St Andrews. [NRS]

THOMSON, JAMES, a farmer in Middle Campsie, father of Beatrix, born 1744, died 1745. [Airlie gravestone, Angus]

THOMSON, JAMES, a gardener at Cortachy, Angus, 1780; husband of Ann Gourlay, parents of Alexander. [NRS.GD16.Sec.41/973] [Cortachy gravestone, Angus]

THOMSON, JOHN, tenant in Tarriebuckle, Lochlee, Angus, 1716. [NRS.E650/4]

THOMSON, JOHN, a workman in Lintrathen, a Jacobite in 1745. [OR.52/166]

THOMSON, JOHN, died 177-, spouse Margaret Kinloch, died 1806. [Airlie gravestone, Angus]

THOMSON, MARGARET, servant to Lord Aboyne, later in Kirktoun of Aboyne, testament, 8 February 1798, Comm. Aberdeen. [NRS]

THOMSON, MARGARET, only daughter of Andrew Thomson of Banchory, testament, 14 January 1800, Comm. Aberdeen. [NRS]

THOMSON, ROBERT, son of George Thomson a merchant in Aberdeen, educated at Marischal College, minister of Lethnot, Angus, from 1685 to 1716, husband of Anna Lindsay. [F.5.399]

THOMSON, THOMAS, tenant in Tomnarraw, Lordship of Mar, Aberdeenshire, 1716. [NRS.E646.2.1]

THOMSON, THOMAS, in the parish of Kindrochit, Lordship of Mar, Aberdeenshire, 1716. [NRS.E646.2.2]

THOMSON, JAMES, a farmer in Middle Campsie, father of Beatrix, born 1744, died 1745. [Airlie MI]

THOMSON, JAMES, a gardener at Cortachy, 1780; husband of Ann Gourlay, parents of Alexander. [NRS.GD16.Sec.41/973] [Cortachy gravestone]

THOMSON, JOHN, tenant in Tarriebuckle, Lochlee, 1716. [NAS.E650/4]

THOMSON, JOHN, died 177-, spouse Margaret Kinloch, died 1806. [Airlie gravestone]

THOMSON, ROBERT, son of George Thomson a merchant in Aberdeen, educated at Marischal College, minister of Lethnot, Angus, from 1685 to 1716, husband of Anna Lindsay. [F.5.399]

THOMSON, THOMAS, tenant in Tomnarraw, Lordship of Mar, Aberdeenshire, 1716. [NRS.E646.2.1]

THOMSON, THOMAS, in the parish of Kindrochit, Lordship of Mar, Aberdeenshire, 1716. [NRS.E646.2.2]

THOMSON, WILLIAM, born 1763, minister at Strachan, died 18 November 1807. [Strachan gravestone]

THOW, JOHN, tenant in Turnabrain, Lochlee, Angus, 1716. [NRS.E650/4]

THOW, JOHN, tenant in Arsellach, Lochlee, Angus 1716. [NRS.E650/4]

TINDAL, WILLIAM, tenant of Blackmill, husband of Margaret Valentine, parents of Anne, David, and Isabel. [Edzell gravestone, Angus]

TODD, ALEXANDER, tenant in Kedloch, Lochlee, Angus, 1716. [NRS.E650/4]

TOSH, ALEXANDER, minister at Tarland, Aberdeenshie, a sasine, 1740. [NRS.RS29.VI.468]

TOSH, DAVID, in Oldtoun, Lethnot, Angus, 1716, 1722. [NRS.E650/4; CH2.628/17]

TOSHACH, JOHN, in Navar, Angus, 1726. [NRS.CH2.628/17]

TOSHACH, ROBERT, in Navar, Angus, 1726. [NRS.CH2.628/17]

TREW, HENRY, born 1792, late Colonial Secretary of Dominica, died at Grove Cottage, Banchory, Aberdeenshire, on 29 March 1884. [Banchory-Ternan gravestone]

TROUP, JOHN, son of John Troup a blacksmith in Banchory, was apprenticed to George Beet a blacksmith in Aberdeen, for 5 years, 28 November 1788, Cautioner – George Troup, a square wright in Banchory. [ACA]

TULLO, GEORGE, husband of Jean Enderdeal born 1713, died 1773, parents of David, Katherine, George, John, Alexander, and James. [Lethnot gravestone, Angus]

TULLY, DAVID, an apprentice to Andrew Davidson a tailor in Lethnot, Angus, 1758. [NRS.CH2.628/1/172]

TURING, Reverend ALEXANDER, born 1701, minister of Oyne, died 24 August 1782. [Oyne gravestone]

TYTLER, ALEXANDER, son of William Tytler a farmer in Strachan, Kincardineshire, was apprenticed to James Gammel a merchant in Greenock, for three years, in 1778. [NRS.GD1.500.68]

TYTLER, GEORGE, born 1706, educated at Marischal College, minister of Fern, Angus, from 1745 to his death in 1785, husband of Janet Robertson, parents of Barbara, George, Mary, James and Henry William. [F.5.397]

TYTLER, JAMES, born in 1745, son of Reverend George Tytler, a balloonist and editor of the *Encyclopedia Britannica,* died in Massachusetts, in 1805. [F.5.397]

VALENTINE, DAVID, tenant in Tillydovie, Navar and Lethnot, Angus,1770. [NRS.CH2.628/17/14]

VEITCH, CHARLES, of Glen Isla, Angus, was admitted as a burgess of St Andrews in 1743. [St Andrews Burgess Roll]

VEITCH, JAMES, of Glen Isla, a deed, 10 June 1752. [NRS.RD4.178/1.567]

WADDELL, ANDREW, drummer or piper of the 1st Strathspey Fencible Regiment, 1793. [NRS.GD248.463.1]

WALKER, ALEXANDER, born 1758, tenant in Arlar, died 1795, husband of Mary Forbes, born 1752, died 1796, parents of Sarah, and Andrew. [Birse gravestone, Aberdeenshire]

WALKER, ALEXANDER, born 1761, tenant in East Mill of Kenalty, Angus, died 1815, husband of Martha Ferguson. [Cortachy gravestone, Angus]

WALKER, WILLIAM, a taxpayer in Mains of Glenbucket, 1799. [ACA]

WATSON, CHARLES, born 1779, inn-keeper at Castletown of Braemar, died 1825, son of John Watson and his wife Catherine Craig. [Braemar gravestone, Aberdeenshire]

WATSON, JAMES, factor of the Mar estate in Aberdeenshire, 1715-1717. [NRS.E646.57]

WATSON, JOHN, born 1715, died at Blackhill, Angus, in 1796. [Airlie gravestone, Angus]

WATSON, JOHN, born 1734, innkeeper, died 1811, spouse Catherine Craig, born 1746, died 1825, son James Watson, born 1774, died 1795. [Braemar gravestone, Aberdeenshire]

WATSON, JOHN, a taxpayer in Castleton, Crathie, 1799. [ACA]

WATT, ALEXANDER, died 1788, husband of Isabella Gray, died 1832. [Banchory Devenick gravestone, Aberdeenshire]

WATT, DAVID, born 1661, resident of Dykehead, died 1741. [Cortachy gravestone, Angus]

WATT, JOHN, born 1739, tenant in Cullow, died 1836, husband of Janet Shaw, born 1745, died 1819. [Cortachy gravestone, Angus]

WAUGH, JOHN, born 1756, minister of Menmuir, Angus, from 1783 to his death in 1824, husband of Frances Elisabeth Gregory. [F.5.408]

WEBSTER, DAVID, in Lackethead, Cortachy, Angus, testament, 1731, Comm. Brechin. [NRS]

WEBSTER, GEORGE, a workman in Kingoldrum, a Jacobite in 1745. [OR.53][P.3.396]

WEBSTER, JAMES, tenant in Burn of Coals, Lochlee, Angus, 1716. [NRS.E650/4]

WEMYSS, GEORGE, graduated MA from St Andrews in 1690, minister of Fern, Angus, from 1698 to his death in 1737, husband of Marjory Spalding, parents of Robert and James. [F.5.396]

WEMYSS, JAMES, minister of Fern, Angus, from 1735 to 1744. [F.5.397]

WHYTE, ALEXANDER, born 1753, died 1817. [Clova gravestone, Angus]

WHYTE, JOHN, a tenant in Auchosie, Lethnot, Angus, 1716. [NRS.E650/4]

WHITE, JOHN, a workman in Kingoldrum, a Jacobite in 1745. [OR.54]

WILKIE, JOHN, a workman in Nether Campsie, Lintrathen, a Jacobite in 1745. [OR.54]

WILL, CHARLES, born 1743, farmer in Tillybardin, died 1828, husband of Elizabeth Bowman, born 1779, died 1823. [Lethnot gravestone, Angus]

WILL, ROBERT, servant to Robert Donaldson, in Drustie, Lochlee, Angus, testament, 1753, Comm. Brechin. [NRS]

WILLIAMSON, WILLIAM, born 1741, farmer at the Burn of Pheppie, died 25 March 1814, husband of Jean Milne, born 1741, died 9 February 1778, parents of James, Christian, and William. [Banchory Devenick gravestone, Aberdeenshire]

WILLOCK, JOHN, born 1768, farmer at Bonfarry, died 1827. [Edzell gravestone, Angus]

WILSON, JAMES, born at Brae of Auldallan 1756, to Hilton in 1806, died 1830, husband of Ann Smith, born 1768, died 1830. [Lintrathen gravestone, Angus]

WILSON, WILLIAM, a farmer in Dalarin, died 1769, husband of Isobel Thom who died 1782, parents of John, William, and Jane. [Glen Prosen gravestone, Angus]

WINTER, CHARLES, in Aucharn, Angus, a sasine, 1771. [NRS.RS35.23.224]

WINTER, JAMES, born 1660, died Peathaugh, Glen Isla, Angus, in 1732. [Cortachy gravestone, Angus]

WRIGHT, JOHN, a workman in Kingoldrum, a Jacobite in 1745. [OR.55]

WRIGHT, JOHN, a servant in Lindertis, Airlie, a Jacobite in 1745. [OR.56]

WYLLIE, GEORGE, tenant in Auchintoul, Lochlee, Angus, 1716. [NRS.E650/4]

WYLLIE, JAMES, tenant in Tilliarblet, Angus, testaments, 1744, 1757; relict Jean Molison, testament 1744, Comm. Brechin. [NRS]

WYLLIE, THOMAS, born 1728, farmer in the Mains of Edzell, died 1795, husband of Isobel Black, died 1790. [Edzell gravestone, Angus]

YOUNG, ALEXANDER, a workman in Balintore, Lintrathen, a Jacobite in 1745, [OR.56]

YOUNG, CHARLES, born 1712, died 1775, husband of Euphan Rob, born 1714, died 1784; tenant in North Bridgend of Cortachy, 1752. [Cortachy gravestone, Angus] [NRS.GD16.Sec.28/354]

YOUNG, CHARLES, born 1747, farmer in Tillifumrey, died 1816, his sister Catherine Young, born 1750, died 1800, brother Harry Young, born 1745, died 1807. [Birse gravestone, Aberdeenshire]

YOUNG, JAMES, born 1721, a dyer at East Mill of Cortachy, died 1796, husband of Elizabeth Low, born 1739, died 1803. [Cortachy gravestone, Angus]

YOUNG, JOHN, master of the Charity school at Clachturn, 1720. [NRS.GD95.14.15]

YOUNG, JOHN, in Nether Migby, Kinnordy, Angus, 1755. [NRS.GD205.29.239]

YOUNG, WILLIAM, Corporal of the 1st Strathspey Fencible Regiment, 1793. [NRS.GD248.463.1]

www.ingramcontent.com/pod-product-compliance
Lightning Source LLC
Chambersburg PA
CBHW050843160426
43192CB00011B/2127